Pg 84, 28, 30, 31, 32, 43, 44, 45, 51, 61, 62, 73, 74, 95
97, 117, 118, 131 91st, copyright form info Pg 225-229
and getting a copyright
PLANTSCAPING Pg 131; Book DROPSHIP Directory $7.00 Pg 233

D1559536

STAY HOME
AND
MAKE MONEY
BY
Russ von Hoelscher

ISBN: 0-940398-17-6

This book is dedicated with love to two special ladies in my life: my mother, Francis Hoelscher Dimmerman, and my aunt, Mildred ("Milly") Hoelscher.

TABLE OF CONTENTS

SECTION ONE: How to Establish a Home Business that is Right for You

Is any "Type" of Home Business
  Right for You... 5
Test Your Personal Skills 6
Your Plan.. 7
Your Attitude 9
Business Records.. 10
Choosing Your Home Business 15
Some Examples of a "Product" Business 16
Some Examples of a "Home Service" Business 16
Some Examples of a "Home-Based Service"
  Business 16
Ten Commandments of Establishing a Successful
  Home Business 17
Zoning Restrictions 18
Make a Positive Statement........................... 20
Pricing Your Product or Service 21
Basic Supplies & Equipment 22
Obtaining a DBA/Business License 23
A Business Checking Account......................... 23
Build Repeat Business 23
How to Effectively Manage Your Time 24
How Much Money is Needed.......................... 25
Marketing & Promotion 26
Government Help...................................... 28
Checklists for Home Business Owners 33

SECTION TWO: Profitable Home Business Opportunities

Successful Garage Sales 37
Decide What You Will Sell. 37
What Items Can be Sold at a Garage Sale 38
Plan for Success 40
Display and Labeling 41
Cleanliness Brings More Cash. 42
Others Items to Have Available. 43
Advertising 43
Newspapers Ads 44
How to Entice Customers to Get Out of Their Cars
    and Walk Up to Your Garage Sale 45
Selling Tips 46
How Much Money Will Your Sale Bring 47
Making Money at Flea Markets and Swap Meets 49
Draw Customers to Your Booth 51
Cashing In on Your Bright Ideas. 53
Ask Yourself Questions 54
Know What to Invent. 54
Making Money Through Sale or License 55
How to Find Someone to Market Your Idea
    or Invention. 56
Who to Talk to 57
Turn Rejection into Acceptance 58
How to go Into Business With Your Invention 58
Getting Started Right 60
Get Some Expert Help 61
How to Protect Your Inventions 61
How to Protect Your Ideas 63
How to Submit an Idea to a Company 63
How to Make Money as a Free-lance Consultant 65
Finding Customers for Your Consulting Practice...... 67
Make Money with a Microcomputer 70
Selecting Your Microcomputer 71
Publishing Your Own Software. 75
Selling Microcomputers 76
Source Directory Computer Manufacturers 77
    MLM—Network Marketing—a Home-Based
    Business with Great Potential 85

Selecting the Guys Who Wear the "White Hats" 85
Select a Good Product 86
The Multi-Level Concept. 87
The Sky's the Limit 88
Beware of ILlegal Products 88
Get the Facts and Figures from "The Horse's
   Mouth" 89
MLM Books 90
The Magazine of the Industry 91
Home Typing. 91
Hotline: Telephone Profits 93
Pay Phone Profits. 94
Claim Your Share of the Twenty-Five
   Billion-Dollar Opportunity 95
Important Dates 97
Fancy Writing for Fancy Profits. 97
Questions & Answers Bureau 98
Cash for Cartoons 98
Sell a Cartoon Course. 99
Entertainment Bureau 100
Inventors Rep 101
Vocational Counseling 102
Braid Rugs. 103
Design Hats 104
Furniture Upholstering 104
Art & Craft Brokerage 105
Grow Organic Vegetables. 106
Flower Power Profits 107
Kitchen Candy Profits 108
Oriental Rugs 110
Rent Fences 110
Golden Profits from the Golden Gate 111
Wealth-Build with Log Homes 112
Make Big Bux in the Blooming Health Field 112
Believe it or not: They Pay for Dust 113
Vinyl Repair Profits 114
Let the IRS Help You Make Money 115
Be a Consumer Hero 116
Video Tape Special Occasions 116
Blow Up Your Profits. 117
Coupon Clipping 118

Seminars in the Home 119
Transportation & Lodging Exchanges 122
Private Airplanes 122
Moving Together.................................122
Buying and Selling Almost Anything 124
Important Buying Guidelines 125
Pyramid Your Profits............................127
Profits from Plants.............................127
Gourmet Profits from Catering 131
Delivery Service Success.........................134
Making Money with Toys 136
Boarding Pets 139
Pony Picture Profits............................140
Big Business in Babysitting 141
Typesetting.....................................142
Home Retailing 144
Protesting Profits 147
Making and Repairing Dolls 149
Top Hat and Tail 152
Fossil Finding 154
How to Start an Entrepreneur Club 156
Home Business Franchises.......................159

SECTION THREE: Writing and/or Self-Publishing Success

Writing...169
Finding Subjects to Write About 169
Profit from Magazine Articles 176
What Editors Want..............................177
Marketing Articles 179
Methods of Book Publishing......................185
Self-Publishing 188
Is Self-Publishing for You 189
Publishing for Profits...........................191
Successful Book Distribution 192
How to Sell Bookstores 193
A 50% Discount Could Swing the Deal 197
Sell Yourself, then Book Dealers.................198
Sell Libraries 198

Selling Words to Big Catalog Houses 199
Big Discounts for Big Shipments 199
Publishing a Newsletter 201
Your Subject Should Relate to Your Interests 202
Format 202
Overall Newsletter Cost 202
Repeat Profits 203
More Letters for Cash 205
Credit & Collection Writing Service 205
Operate a Hobby Letter 206
Family Name Letter 206
Resume Profits 203
Resume Writing Factors 208
Soliciting Resume Clients 210
Shopper Profits 212
Repeat Business 214
Sell Information 217
Speak Out for Profits 219
Writing & the Law 221
Protect Your Property with a Copyright 223
What Can You Copyright 225
Step-by-Step Guide 228
When They Won't Pay 230
Ghost Writing Help 231
Writing and Publishing Resources 232

SECTION FOUR: How to Make Big Money in Mail Order

Mail Order is Booming 243
You Can Start Part-Time 243
What About Competition 244
How Much Money is Needed 244
Your Own Products or Someone Else's 245
Markup 246
Getting Started on a Shoestring 247
Step-by-Step Examples 247
Effective Two-Step Mail Selling 250
Checking Profits 251
Mail Order Space Advertising 253

Testing and Perfecting 253
Inflated Ad Rates 254
The Best Months to Run Display Ads 254
Don't Confuse Cover Date with On Sale Date 255
Effective Print Media 256
Direct Mail Advertising 258
Almost Instant Results 259
Good Copy is a Must 259
Mailing Lists 260
12 Direct Mail Success Tips 260
The Proven Direct Mail Format 262
Finding Products to Sell 265
Recommended Books 266

SOURCE GUIDE 267
Recommended Reading 269
Important Directories 271
Special Publication Offers 272
Free Goodies 273

INTRODUCTION

Making money at home is now a reality to many millions of Americans, Canadians, and other people all over the world. Predictions on how many of us will soon be engaged in work at home boggle the imagination. The U.S. Labor Department believes that up to half of all Americans could be working at home by the year 2000. If their prediction comes to pass, obviously a great number of these home workers will be home-based employees of various major corporations. Millions and millions of others, however, will be home-based entrepreneurs, engaged in a business of their very own. My book is addressed to you, the present or future home business entrepreneur!

Stay Home and Make Money was written for today's independent home business entrepreneur and for the countless numbers of women and men who are now seeking a profitable home business. This new book will help make your success dream come true.

Stay Home and Make Money will give you the important guidelines you must employ to establish any type of home business. Beyond that, this book will present you with a heaping smorgasbord of home business opportunities to choose from. You can make money, lots of money, by either copying the success of others, or by starting a very unique business that you have created. For most people, copying success is easier than creating success.

History does seem to be repeating itself. Although we have entered the hi-tech age of information and automation, we seem to be, at the same time, reverting back to a "cottage industry society" which was prominent over 100 years ago. Estimates vary, and exact data is not available but there are probably at least over twenty-five million people working at home today (1987-88) and the number is growing rapidly.

The majority are part-timers but the ranks of the full-time entrepreneurs are rapidly increasing.

In addition to offering you a rich buffet of home money-making opportunities, I have included only those wealth-building opportunities that can be launched with little or no start-up capital. This is a book loaded with high profit plans that do not require huge investments.

If you have an ounce of creativity, and a pound of burning desire for success, you can still make a ton of money regardless of prevailing economic conditions. And this book will help!

This book is divided into four sections:

Section One: How to Establish a Home Business
that is Right for You
Section Two: Profitable Home Business Opportunities
Section Three: Writing and/or Self-Publishing Success
Section Four: How to Make Big Money in Mail Order

In addition to these four sections, a helpful Source Guide is found in the back of the book.

Full-time or spare-time, if you want to establish a money-making home enterprise or quickly expand one that you already have launched, this book is here to help you do it!

You deserve Total Success,

Russ von Hoelscher

SECTION ONE:

How to Establish a Home Business that is Right for You

Section I in this book is important. Please don't skip it in your haste to check out the many opportunities presented in the other sections.

You must learn before you earn. In this initial section you will learn the basic tenets to establishing a business at home.

Regardless of which type or types (some people operate several home businesses simultaneously) of home business you choose to operate, there is a right way and a wrong way to set up your business, and time-tested techniques to keep it running smoothly.

This first section of *Stay Home and Make Money* will help you organize and establish your business for maximum efficiency.

HOW TO ESTABLISH YOUR OWN HOME BUSINESS

There are many thousands of home business, money-making activities to choose from. Before you pick the one that suits your skills and temperament best (and keep in mind, many home business entrepreneurs *do* get involved in more than just one venture at the same time), first you must prepare yourself for the success you desire.

IS ANY TYPE OF HOME BUSINESS RIGHT FOR YOU?

This is the basic question, and only you have the answer. Do you fully understand your individual strengths and limitations? Are you a self-starter? It is essential that you be able to manage your time and work productively without someone telling you what to do. You should also be able to organize your schedule and work, take charge of things, and finish the projects that you start.

Unlike businesses on Main Street, which often fail due to under-capitalization, the majority of home businesses that fail (and well over 50% *do* fail) do so because of poor management. You can start many types of home business with very little money, but you must supply the desire, the

5

persistence, and the management.

If you have great desire and are determined to see it through, but do need help in management areas, you may wish to hone these skills at one of the alternative education or adult night school classes which are offered in most cities throughout the country.

TEST YOUR PERSONAL SKILLS

The following self-starter and personal management test will tell you (if you answer questions honestly, that is) where your capabilities and limitations are, and what areas you must seek improvement in.

(1) Are you a self-starter? Do you like to make decisions and set objectives? ☐ Yes ☐ No

(2) Are you comfortable "working alone" on a project from start to finish? ☐ Yes ☐ No

(3) Are you good at organizing your work? ☐ Yes ☐ No

(4) Are you basically self-confident? ☐ Yes ☐ No

(5) Are you an individual who prefers not having a boss? ☐ Yes ☐ No

(6) Are you willing to work harder for yourself than you would working for another? ☐ Yes ☐ No

(7) Are you willing to do research, reading, and inside or outside classroom study to perfect certain business skills? ☐ Yes ☐ No

(8) Do you believe you can be successful in your own home business? ☐ Yes ☐ No

(9) Are you ready to get started right now? ☐ Yes ☐ No

(10) Do you desire more personal and financial independence? ☐ Yes ☐ No

6

Without making "right or wrong" judgements, I feel a good candidate for a home business should answer *yes* to at least seven out of these ten questions. And a positive yes answer to questions 1, 8, and 10 are very important. Management and organizational skills can be developed. Desire and determination should be present at the start.

YOUR PLAN

Your business plan gives you an important roadmap to follow to success. Plans are roughed in, altered, amended, updated and corrected. This is an understandable process. The refining of plans comes about as each stage is adjusted to fit the overall pattern. First things first. What kind of business do you want? Basically there are only two—product and service. Do you have a product? Can you perform a needed service? Occasionally the two can be combined.

Self-evaluation will help answer the question of what kind of business.

Why are you going into business for yourself? Do you want to prove a point to yourself or someone else? Motivation of this type can be very strong. Proper planning, as in any endeavor, can make it so. But the reason for striking out on your own is a powerful factor and should be analyzed carefully. It may be the most important reason for success or failure. Plan your steps so that the reason becomes a reinforcing lever rather than an albatross around your neck. There is no reason more powerful than self-motivation. You have decided that you can make a better life for yourself and your family if you can be your own boss. You take the first step. Having taken the step, begun planning, you will find each succeeding step a little easier. Many men have gone into business for themselves simply because they couldn't continue working under conditions they considered intolerable.

Whatever the reason, it is important. It is your drive and incentive. Cultivate it and be sure it will grow. If it fades or wanes you will not put the utmost effort into becoming successful. Reinforcement can be had from friends, family or spouse. Let them be a part of your planning; their enthusiasm will perk you up when your spirits lag.

If you're married you must include your spouse in your plan. He or she can play a vital role as a helpmate. Even if your husband or wife won't be actively helping you run your home business, you need their support and understanding.

It's important also to decide exactly what it is you want from your business: extra income for yourself and the family, or do you want to establish a business that will eventually offer unlimited profit potential? Sometimes a spare-time extra-income venture evolves into a big profit, full-fledged business, but good early planning could make it happen a lot sooner.

Your plans should include growth potential and future expansion in your market. You should plan for gradual increases in personal benefits with large portions of the profits going back into the business to provide for future growth.

Regardless of whether you operate your business yourself or with employees (and most home business owners use "outside help"—often called "independent contractors," when assistance is needed), the formative period may demand long hours and hard work for you. Your design for the modus operandi will necessarily include direct contact with similar business for research into methods which have been used successfully and an insight into questionable practices which may be detrimental to the goals which you seek.

First in importance is your ability to physically stand up to the hours and strains. Much as an athlete prepares himself for the competition, the new entrepreneur must also prepare both physically and mentally. Singleness of purpose is a state of mind which must be entered into by training; physical preparedness is a critical part of that training. To be unprepared to meet the rigors and responsibilities of the new enterprise is to invite defeat. The old saw "anything worth doing is worth doing well" may sound trite, but the truth cannot be denied. The marathon runner trains intently for the event. He knows if he stops short of his goal he cannot pass the baton and the race is lost. The goal of the entrepreneur can also be lost if he does not have the stamina to stick in there and make the full effort. Quitting too soon can cause the failure of a business that just might have made it.

An important part of marketing is placing your product before the public for their consideration. Advertising comes in many forms. Direct mail advertising can be made to appear as a personal approach to the consumer. Plan to investigate the use of mailing lists. Newspapers approach the public in a broad manner but are limited in coverage. If your product has national appeal you will look into magazine coverage.

One important method of advertising your business comes under the heading of PR—public relations. The term PR covers a multitude of sins. A favorable article in the local newspaper is worth its weight in gold. But there is more to PR than the old concept of the press agent. Direct telephone approach should also be considered.

YOUR ATTITUDE

A successful home business calls for a positive, "can do" attitude. You must believe in yourself, and in your product or service. Set big goals and become determined to see your money-making plans become reality. Overcoming obstacles —and you will have your share—with true determination to succeed is essential.

Remember:

IF YOU THINK YOU ARE BEATEN...
   YOU ARE;

IF YOU THINK YOU DARE NOT,
  YOU DON'T.
IF YOU LIKE TO WIN, BUT THINK YOU CAN'T,
  IT'S ALMOST A CINCH YOU WON'T.
IF YOU THINK YOU'LL LOSE,
  YOU'RE LOST.
FOR OUT IN THIS WORLD WE FIND
  SUCCESS BEGINS WITH A FELLOW'S WILL;
  IT'S ALL IN THE STATE OF MIND.
LIFE'S BATTLES DON'T ALWAYS GO
  TO THE STRONGER OR FASTER MAN;
BUT SOONER OR LATER THE MAN THAT WINS
  IS THE ONE WHO THINKS HE CAN.

BUSINESS RECORDS

Keeping good business records can be a laborious, often boring task to the entrepreneur. Nevertheless, it is very important.

In the beginning I mentioned mismanagement accounted for an extremely high rate of failure among new home businesses. Lack of records or slipshod record-keeping is probably the most blatant form of mismanagement. A business cannot survive unless thorough and accurate records are kept. The simplest but most complete form of business records applicable to your business is the best insurance against failure.

Why do you need to keep records? For the same reason you need a road map for a trip. To tell where you are going, where you are now and where you have been. To repeat a statement I have made several times before, the object is to realize the greatest possible return on your investment. Without records you cannot possibly know if you are over-paying for the operation of your venture. It matters not how large or small the business, the necessity for accurate and complete records is the same.

Taxes are paid on gross receipts less operating expenses. Records are necessary to obtain the very best tax advantage. Inventory control requires records, sufficient control over every phase of the business can only be had with an adequate system of records.

When you first organize your enterprise you will need to keep records of capital outlay, equipment purchased or leased and the terms by which the assets are obtained. Initial inventory and renewal methods as inventory is dispensed requires records. The method of financing the venture must be a matter of record as must be methods of repayment. Cost of financing will be an important part of those records. If yours is a corporate structure the method of issuing stock, the classes of stock and the number of shares plus their par value if any are a part of your financial records.

Bookkeeping is a word many of us shy away from. It is the dull and sometimes frightening side of business. Yet without it no business can survive. For a beginning, each day's transactions must be recorded. The day book or journal serves this purpose. Each receipt for money paid out, each bill for goods received, all memos, each and every written item of the day's business is recorded in the journal. These entries are later transferred to the bookkeeping ledgers.

There are two systems used. The single system and double system, known as single or double entry. Most accountants prefer to set up a double entry. The reason being that in a double entry system errors are more apparent and more easily corrected. In the double entry system bookkeeping each item is entered twice. Once as debit and once as a credit. If you purchase a truck to be used for delivery of your product the expenditure would be entered as a debit against cash on hand and a credit on accounts payable. Thus used the double entry will balance credits against debits. Since the accountant only checks books on a quarterly basis a trial balance is taken at the end of each month by your bookkeeper to assure that the credits and debits do balance. Any error picked up at this point is easier to locate and correct than it would be over a longer period of time.

11

There are two basic systems of keeping accounts. The cash basis is used when neither income nor expense is recorded until the transaction actually takes place. When the bill is paid out or the income is actually received it is recorded in the books. Until that time a file of memos, receipts and bills is kept for future posting. On the other hand, the accrual method records each transaction as it occurs. When a sale is made it is entered as income even though payment has not yet been received. When a purchase is made it is entered immediately even though no cash has been disbursed. There are certain tax advantages to the accrual basis of accounting and in some instances the IRS prefers a business to use the accrual basis.

Books and equipment necessary for setting up proper records vary from business to business. A retail business will require, in most instances, cash registers, adding machines or electronic calculators with printout capability and possibly check and credit card verification equipment. Also required are methods of recording sales, cash received, cash disbursed, employee time records, ledgers and checkbook. Depending on the size and type of operation, the use of petty cash memos, pay slips, statement of accounts of charge customers and special records may be required.

Each day's business should be recorded. Cash sales, payments on accounts receivable and miscellaneous should be entered. When totaled these should be balanced against cash on hand. This should indicate a balance, shortage or overage in cash. Charge sales should be entered to show the total day's transactions.

With exception of the items handled by petty cash, each disbursement should be by check. This gives a record of the transaction, the amount involved and a receipt when the canceled check is returned. When writing checks be certain that a statement, bill or invoice exists to justify the expenditure.

Payroll (which may be payments to "outside help") may be handled by cash or check. If the cash method is used each pay envelope should have a receipt stub to be signed by the employee. Another method is to have the employee sign a payroll book. If payroll is handled by check the stub and canceled check are sufficient receipt. If the work force is large enough you may use an independent payroll service. Where checks are used, frequently a running account of FICA, withholding for state and federal income taxes and other deductibles is entered on the employees stub which keep employer and employee current with regard to deductions from income.

As owner you will withdraw certain amounts from the business on a regular basis as personal income. This is not a salary in the true sense if yours is a proprietorship or partnership and will not be entered in the books as salary. If you are the owner of a corporation you will draw a salary the same as all employees.

Since most home-based businesses are run as sole proprietorships using only "outside help", your ledger will record cash flow, expenses and money taken out of the business. However, the payroll information just given will be important to you if you expand greatly and require regular employees.

An important item of accounting is the profit and loss statement, or P&L sheet. The P&L sheet is done monthly and carried forward from month to month. This results in a financial condition for the year to date. Sort of a State of the Union message, this document allows you to monitor the operation and make changes as necessary to obtain the best results. A profit and loss statement also serves other purposes. It can be presented to a lender to justify a loan for business purposes. A prospective buyer of your business, should you ever decide to sell, will demand a P&L statement to help him decide whether to buy or not.

Most states today have some form of sales or use tax. The method of collecting the tax and recording the collections varies. If your product requires that you add sales tax to your selling price, you will be expected to retain this money

13

and then remit it to the appropriate state agency on a regular basis (usually monthly or quarterly).

As the owner of a business it is essential that you keep a record of any income withdrawn from the business. These records are for the purpose of filing self-employed tax returns to account to the federal and state government.

There are many more records but usually their application is for specific types of enterprises. Your accountant or professional bookkeeper will set up the system most useful for your operation.

As your home business grows, you may want to hire a professional bookkeeping service to help you with your record-keeping. If you file complete information on sales and expenses, a professional bookkeeper can quickly put things in exact order on a monthly, bimonthly or quarterly basis for a modest fee. Then you may wish to visit an accountant once a year to assist you in filing your tax returns.

CHOOSING YOUR HOME BUSINESS

If you're not already engaged in one or more home business activities, it's now time to seriously consider what type of business will be best for you. While there are zillions of possibilities, there are two basic types of home businesses:

(1) Products

(2) Services

Products may be sold that are self-created or self-produced or products can be purchased from other sources (manufacturers, distributors, publishers, etc.) for resale. Service-oriented home businesses fall into two broad categories: (A) services provided for others, strictly at your home, or (B) services provided for others where some or all of your work is outside the home.

If all of your business is produced and provided in your home, you operate a 100% home business. If some of your business is provided outside your home, but your home is *headquarters*, you're operating what could technically be labeled as a *home-based business*. In any case, any business that uses one's home as business headquarters, regardless if all or only part of business activities are performed inside the house or apartment, is usually put in the general category of home business.

SOME EXAMPLES OF A "PRODUCT" BUSINESS

Advertising specialties, antiques, art books and booklets, cookware, cosmetics, crafts, diet and health items, food stuffs, furniture, gifts, greeting cards, herbs, hobby items, household goods, imports, jewelry, kits, office products, perfumes and colognes, posters and prints, plants and flowers, reports and guides, stationery, swap meet and flea market merchandise.

SOME EXAMPLES OF "HOME SERVICE" BUSINESSES

Ad agency, astrology, accounting and bookkeeping, artist, calligraphy, child care, clipping service, computer services, consulting (on practically any subject or business), copywriter, financial advisor, massage, mechanics, organizational specialist, pet care, photography, print brokering, private teaching, private investigations, publicist, researcher, secretarial services, telecommunications, therapist, typesetting, typing, writer.

EXAMPLES OF "HOME-BASED" SERVICE BUSINESSES

Independent sales to businesses
Independent house-to-house sales
Repair and maintenance
Delivery services
Cleaning or remodeling
Photography/video

Operating a home business does not necessarily mean that you will do all of your business within the home. It *does* mean your home is your office and the base of all your business activities.

16

TEN COMMANDMENTS OF ESTABLISHING A SUCCESSFUL HOME BUSINESS

(1) Thou shall plan well

(2) Thou shall set goals

(3) Thou shall be enthusiastic

(4) Thou shall offer a quality service or product

(5) Thou shall always please thy customer

(6) Thou shall carefully manage thy business

(7) Thou shall use thy time wisely—time is money

(8) Thou shall keep expenses low

(9) Thou shall creatively promote thyself and thy business

(10) Thou shall overcome all obstacles on the road to success

ZONING RESTRICTIONS

Although there may be as many as twenty-five million people actively involved in home businesses in America —perhaps even more—a great many of them are doing so in violation of local municipality laws. It's a shame, but many cities and towns across the land have old laws on the books (often laws once written to abolish home-based "sweat shops" that were promiment at the turn of the century) which prohibit or restrict home business activities.

Obviously, many of these local restrictions are being ignored by millions of home business operators. While I cannot tell you to simply forget about all existing laws, I will tell you to check with your local elected officials to see what restrictions, however outdated, are on the books in your area. If no laws prohibit you from doing what you want to do, it's full speed ahead. If there *are* any prohibitive zoning laws, you can do one of three things:

(1) try to get the law changed

(2) move

(3) ignore it

The choice is yours!

If millions are operating home businesses in areas where restrictions to such activity apply (and I'm convinced this is true), how do they do it? Here are two examples:

Frank Tillmanson of Cleveland, Ohio was recently refused a business license because the residential neighborhood he lived in had a zoning restriction against any kind of business. Solution: Frank rented a private mailbox in a business district two miles from his house and reapplied for, and obtained his business license.

Cindy Norstrom of Madison, Wisconsin, was also refused a business license due to old zoning restrictions. She became indignant. "My typing service is a benefit to my customers and harms no one in my neighborhood." She decided to plead her case, fought city hall, and she won!

More often, a business license is granted because no one, not even city hall clerks, realize restrictions apply. In such cases, you probably will never get hassled by city officials unless—and it is a big UNLESS—your home business activities disturb your neighbors. (A young lady here in San Diego was recently evicted from her apartment where she ran a typesetting business because her typesetting machine was quite noisy and she was fond of working past midnight—a situation her fellow apartment dwellers did not take kindly to. Nor did they like the constant stream of customers back and forth to her apartment.)

With any home business, stay on good terms with neighbors, and in most cases, your business should be conducted in a discreet way so that almost no one (except friends, relatives and clients) knows you are running it from your home.

While making your official address a private or postal box is easy, changing existing laws may be a big hassle.

With more and more big corporations expected to employ more home workers, I think many old and outdated zoning laws will change. The big companies have the clout to effect legal changes.

Fortunately, only a few types of home businesses seem to raise the ire of neighbors, who then complain to city officials, who may take action. These are generally businesses that involve heavy traffic.

A few years ago a couple opened a used bookstore in their home in Chula Vista, California, and were soon ordered to close because neighbors did not like all the foot traffic or the automobiles that constantly were parking in front of their houses from 11 a.m. to 8 p.m.

If your home business will not produce a flow of traffic and large delivery trucks, and most do not, it should bring little or no attention to neighbors, and thereby result in no community hassles.

MAKE A POSITIVE STATEMENT ABOUT YOURSELF AND YOUR BUSINESS

Just because it's a home business doesn't mean it's not a real business. It must still be run in a positive and professional manner. If customers will be coming into your home, your home (or at least the areas visible to them) must be kept neat and clean. You should also greet people in a professional way and be dressed appropriately. No robes, pajamas, or housecoats!

Arrange to have an answering machine or answering service take the calls you can't personally handle. If you have small children, never allow them to answer your business telephone. A little rug rat who answers the phone and then yells "Daddy (or "Mommy"), it's for you," will be making a statement about your business, but it might not be the one you want to make.

If all or part of your business will be conducted by mail, and almost all businesses use the mails to one extent or another, make sure your stationery (letterheads, envelopes, circulars, etc.) are attractively typeset and printed. Forget about those messy rubber stamps. The extra money you pay for quality will pay for itself, over and over again.

The way you conduct yourself, in person, on the phone, and with your printed literature, makes a statement about you and your product or service. Make sure it is a positive one.

Never apologize for operating your business from the home. Rather, emphasize the positive aspects of home operation: you get more done, in less time; you save driving time and gas; low overhead allows you to charge less, etc.

PRICING YOUR PRODUCT OR SERVICE

The lower overhead of a home business will often allow you to price your services and/or products at less money than if you opened an office or shop on Main Street. If this is true for you, very well and good. However, don't grossly underprice your services or products (over the years, your author has found a majority of home business entrepreneurs underprice rather than overprice their wares or services).

Sometimes your customers, if they realize you conduct all or part of your business in your own home, will try to brow-beat you into a much cheaper price. This happened to Barbara, a professional masseuse in San Diego. After working five years for an exclusive health spa, she decided to go into business for herself at home. Because she was very talented in giving facials and full body massages, clients old and new began to call on her—some of whom expected to pay much less than the 25% discount off the spa's substantial fees. When Barbara realized that many people thought her *at home* prices should be up to one-half off spa rates, she used a marketing ploy to set her clients straight. She told them, "At 25% off the spa's fees, I believe my home fee is reasonable. However, I'm willing to come to your home at the very same price you'd pay to go to the spa." Barbara says most of her clients decided to get her lower home price.

Don't allow clients to use the "you work at home, you should be able to charge much less" tactic to make you lower your prices. Beat them to the punch. When discussing your fees, tell them (if they already know you're a home business person) that your fee already reflects your lower overhead.

Mary Jane Allbright of Rochester, New York, told me that some of her bookkeeping clients asked about lower fees when she moved from a downtown Rochester, New York office building to her condo in the suburbs. "What savings?" she answers. "My brother, the real estate developer, owned that building and gave me free rent. It may be more pleasant for me to work at home, but it will probably cost me *more* money!"

BASIC SUPPLIES AND EQUIPMENT

While specific supplies and equipment will be required by every individual home business, here are 12 essentials that will be required by everyone:

1. a desk and chair
2. file cabinet
3. envelopes, letterheads, and other printed matter
4. typewriter
5. storage area/folding table
6. miscellaneous office supplies (rubber bands, paperclips, envelope openers, glue, typewriter correction fluid, etc.)
7. a large wastebasket
8. proper lighting
9. postage stamps
10. checking account
11. a bookkeeping system
12. a telephone

OBTAINING A D.B.A.
AND/OR A BUSINESS LICENSE

In most cities and towns you will need a "D.B.A." (doing business as) if you use a business name other than your own last name. Also, most municipalities require all types of businesses to be licensed. The cost is almost always very modest and the procedure is a simple one. Call your local city or county clerks office to obtain details on exactly what is required in your area.

A BUSINESS CHECKING ACCOUNT

Once you establish your D.B.A. and secure a business license (if one is required in your locality), it's time to open your business checking account. Hopefully, you will soon be depositing a large number of checks from your customers. If there are several banks in your area, take some time to check them out individually. You are looking for one that charges the lowest service charges, charge per check written, etc. All banks are not the same. Comparison shopping could save you $100 or even more per year in banking fees.

BUILD REPEAT BUSINESS

Offer products and services that lend themselves to repeat business. It's difficult to build a solid home business on one-shot offers. Give them real value and they'll buy from you again and again. Also, having learned a valuable lesson years ago, I have given it this quotation: *Don't cheat or take advantage of your customer—you'll be the loser. Instead, win success by giving your customers their money's worth. And if you really want great success, **give your customers MORE than their money's worth.*** Not just in price, but in value and service, too!

HOW TO EFFECTIVELY
MANAGE YOUR TIME

With the exception of poor business practices and management, nothing can ruin a home business quicker than sloppy work habits and poor time management.

Time is money. Misuse of time seldom involves an isolated incident; it almost always is part and parcel of a well-established pattern of poor work habits. God knows, changing or reprograming our behavior is not an easy task. Learning to cope with the clock and make it work for us rather than against us is no simple behavior change. The potential pay-off is so beneficial, however, that we must turn destructive, time-wasting habits into rewarding habits that best utilize the precious gift that is time.

Many business people in general, and home business people in particular, have huge piles of papers, envelopes and current work on their desks, somehow assuming the more important matters, like cream, will rise to the top. It just doesn't happen.

An effective means of dealing with your papers, projects, mail, etc., is to go through them and divide them into five categories:

(1) High Priority—Immediate Action
(2) Low Priority
(3) Pending
(4) Reading Matter
(5) Wastebasket

By working on one thing (the most important project) at a time, you will find the time to make your business successful.

Beware of well-meaning but time-consuming relatives and friends. Sometimes when friends and relatives discover you're operating a home business, especially if you're full-time at it, they will place time-consuming demands on you. "Since you're home already, will you help me with this task?" or "Can you run little Mary over to the dentist?", etc. Don't fall for it! Sure, you'll bend a little, and occasionally help out, but no more so than if you worked in an office building.

Conduct your home business just like it's a regular business (which it really is!). Prepare for success, learn more to earn more, choose good services/products and persist. The results will be very self-satisfying.

HOW MUCH MONEY IS NEEDED?

While you must have an answer to the above question, I really can't answer for you. If you start your home business in your spare time while you keep your regular job, you may be able to get started for a very modest amount. Perhaps only a few hundred dollars, or even less. You should walk before you run. Do your financial business-building homework. Realistically estimate all potential costs. Some "seed money" may be required—how much depends on the type of business you choose for yourself.

Many home businesses (including many mentioned in this manual) can be started on a shoestring, or even if you're flat broke. Others need larger amounts of capitalization.

With very few exceptions, it is my belief that you should not go deep in debt just to get started. Direct your attention and energy to the kind of home-based business that fits your personal, psychological and financial abilities.

If you're starting a venture where you will be buying and selling merchandise produced by others, it is wise not to get involved with companies who want you to buy and stockpile substantial amounts of their goods. At least not until you're certain it is quickly saleable to a ready-made market.

As mentioned above, I recommend minimum merchandise stockpiling in the beginning stages, if your new home business is centered around buying goods for resale. I also caution you to beware of getting involved with companies who are financially unsound or who operate in a fashion that may be construed to be unethical or downright illegal.

Extra caution is often required in running a multi-level type business. While multi-level selling is popular today, and has earned fantastic income for many, there are some "bad apples" in the multi-level barrel. If the parent company is financially shaky and folds, you could lose a big investment in time and effort, as well as dollars. If the company is making false claims concerning its products, you could even find yourself involved in a legal hassle. Recently, a few multi-level firms have been legally challenged because of alleged misinformation and unsubstantiated claims in the area of human health.

If you're considering offering products or services that require you to make claims of cures or healings for various human disorders, you absolutely should consult with an attorney to determine if you could be liable for making such claims, even by the act of passing out company literature where such claims are mentioned.

A smart rule of thumb in selling any type of product or service, produced by yourself or some other source, is: get a legal opinion concerning all "benefits" that will be expressed or implied orally, or especially in printed sales literature.

MARKETING AND PROMOTION

How do you determine that there is a market for your service or products? Here are some questions to ask yourself for starters:

(A)   Who and how big is my competition?

(B) How does the competition obtain business?

(C) To whom do they sell?

(D) Is there a clear need for my service or product, not currently being met?

(E) Is my market a local one? Can it be promoted nationally?

(F) Is my market easily reachable (through personal contact, advertising or publicity)?

You must be able to both define a real need for your products and be able to reach the potential customers in a cost-effective manner. Who will your primary customers be—housewives, business people, teens, college students, or senior citizens? You need to know!

At your local library there are many books available about identifying your market. These will also instruct you to interpret the significance of data accumulated in test-marketing a product. Also, these will help you deal with professionals to analyze your market if that should become necessary.

Regardless of the kind of business you begin, success will be virtually impossible without sales. Therefore, for the new small, home business, it is extremely important to generate profitable sales as quickly as possible.

Marketing is a general term which describes advertising and promotion. Advertising and promotion can result in cost-effective methods of building sales, and although they go hand in hand, they are distinctly different ideas.

A product or service promoted is much more easily sold than when it is advertised. Customers are more easily convinced to buy when someone other than the designer or producer recommends the product or service. Spending a large sum of money to publish a half-page advertisement in your local newspaper may not produce as much business as a "news feature" article of the same amount of space or less. Good promotion pays big dividends, and the most effective promotion is often good media publicity. It's cost-effective and usually influences more people than costly straight advertising. Promoting your products and services with the help of other individuals or companies can bring quick, satisfying results, as can promoting them and yourself through "publicity" in the media.

I strongly suggest that everyone planning to launch their own home business, get their hands on a copy of Dr. Jeffrey Lant's revealing book, _The Unabashed Self-Promoter's Guide,_ ($30.00 plus $1.50 postage from JLA Publications, 50 Follen St., Suite 507, Cambridge, MA 02138). This is, by far, the best book available on how to manipulate the media and obtain free publicity for your products or services. Throughout this remarkable book, Lant's message is clear: the news media have great power, and they use it very subjectively. But you can get them to use their vast powers of persuasion in your behalf if you understand how the game is played. This book tells you how to plan and win!

GOVERNMENT HELP

Let's consider some positive things government provides to small businesses.

The Small Business Administration (SBA) has a multi-tiered definition of a Small Business. In the broadest sense, the SBA defines a small business as one that is "independently owned and operated and is not dominant in its field." More precisely, the SBA sets forth specific numerical standards as the basis for its definition, depending on the industry in question. For example, a manufacturing small business may have not more than 1500 employees, depending on the business. A wholesaling business may not do business in excess of 22 million dollars, depending again, on the industry. A service business must not exceed $2 million to $8

28

million, depending on the kind of business, and so on. These definitions, in addition to detailed credit requirements and terms under which loans will be made, are spelled out in an SBA publication entitled *Business Loans from the SBA*, available from your local SBA office.

Remember three guidelines that determine whether you and your business will qualify for SBA loan assistance:

(1) unable to get financing from the private sector, from banks

(2) independently owned and operated, not dominant in your field

(3) satisfy requirements pertaining to "small business" as laid down by SBA.

An SBA Loan Guarantee Plan calls for a commercial bank to loan a local entrepreneur X number of dollars, that is guaranteed by the SBA up to 90%. Such a loan is called an *SBA 7(a) Loan*, and usually amounts to no more than $350,000, requiring six to ten years to repay. Interest is less than that generally imposed by commercial banks, although this and other terms and conditions of the 7(a) loan will be determined by your commercial bank working with the SBA.

Normally, the SBA encourages budding home-business entrepreneurs to apply first for loans from the private sector, especially from local banks, before considering the SBA. If unsuccessful at obtaining a bank loan, the entrepreneur will be faced with the task of convincing the Government of the viability of the planned business. The applicant will have to demonstrate trustworthiness, competency and reliability in managing his/her business.

Both private commercial banks and the SBA believe a person should have a personal stake in a developing business, and rightly so. Consequently, the SBA will make a loan for as much as 80% of your initially required capital, while the bank will loan as much as 50%.

Processing loan applications takes time. Generally, a bank is a good deal quicker than the SBA, which may need one or two months. Moreover, SBA loans come complete with Government "guidelines," stating exactly how you are to use the money. One SBA requirement will be that you submit financial statements to the SBA from time to time. Be prudent, be careful, be thorough.

In recent years, SBA has not been readily available to very many home business operators. However, women and minorities, in particular, continue to have some success in securing SBA loans. Still, you have nothing to lose (except the time, effort and costs put into making your presentation) on attempting to get a loan.

The U.S. Small Business Administration, Office of Management Assistance, offers dozens of publications called Management Aids (MA's), Small Marketers Aids (SMA's), and Small Business Bibliographies (SBB's). SMA titles include *Checklist for Going Into Business; Steps in Meeting Your Tax Obligations; Budgeting in a Small Service Firm; Insurance Checklist for Small Business,* and *Public Relations for Small Business.* Examples of SBB's include such winsome titles as *Home Businesses; Market Research Procedures; Training for Small Business;* and *Marketing for Small Business.* Examples of MA's include *Keep Pointed Toward Profit; Finding a New Product for Your Company; Business Plan for Small Manufacturers; Basic Budgets for Profit Planning;* and *Can You Make Money With Your Idea Or Invention?* Consult some of these. All can be obtained by visiting your local SBA office or calling toll-free, 1-800-433 -7212 (in Texas call 1-800-792-8901). You may write to the U.S. Small Business Administration, P.O. Box 15454, Fort Worth, Texas 76119. Refer to your telephone book, under U.S. Government for the telephone number and address of your local SBA office.

The SBA also publishes a number of other helpful pieces of literature. *Your Business and the SBA* describes this government organization, defines Small Business and the responsibilities of the SBA toward small business, describes the kinds of financial assistance available to small business (numbering approximately 25 different kinds of loan plans), sets forth a means of procuring assistance, and addresses the particular needs of women and other minority groups. The SBA has more than 100 field offices open to handle your problems. You can arrange for an appointment with anyone of more than 4400 employees who make up this organization. There is no charge to you for SBA counseling service.

To assist the individual entrepreneur, the SBA has recruited the services of retired business executives. SCORE, Service Corps of Retired Executives, is comprised of men and women skilled in the multifaceted practices of business. They may be helpful to you in providing free management counseling. Available literature quotes 300 SCORE chapters in our 50 states, and Puerto Rico, made up of some 5800 volunteers. SCORE volunteers will give you advice on all aspects of business, from accounting to record-keeping; from merchandising to taxes. SCORE also sponsors pre-business workshops which will familiarize you with the process of beginning a home business. Make note to investigate this free resource.

FREE BUSINESS ADVISE

A very interesting feature has recently been devised and instituted by the Federal Government to aid and assist the small businessperson in the procurement of work. This system is known as PASS, or the Procurement Automated Source System. PASS is a high-tech, computerized network which will allow registered small businesses to be reviewed for consideration upon request from a Federal procuring office or purchasing agent. In other words, if you wish to be considered for Federal contracts and subcontracts, you simply register your company with PASS. Computer identification of your firm is made whenever work of an appropriate nature comes along. Four basic requirements are in order: 1) you are a small firm, independently owned, operated, and managed for profit; 2) if you are a service industry that average annual receipts of 3 preceding years total no more than $2 million; 3) if you are an R&D (research and development) or manufacturing firm, that you employ no more than 500; 4) if you are a general construction firm,

ADDRESS NEXT PAGE

that average annual receipts for 3 preceding years total no more than $12 million. PASS is responsive to businesses owned by women and other minorities. Write for more information to U.S. Small Business Administration, 1441 L Street, NW, Washington, DC 20416.

The IRS provides a very valuable publication entitled, *Index to Tax Publications,* which is thorough and current. It is obtainable by writing to the U.S. Government Printing Office, Superintendent of Documents, Washington, DC 20402, Stock No. 048-004-01695-8, or visit your nearest IRS office. Examples of titles included in this publication are: *Your Federal Income Tax; Circular E—Employer's Tax Guide; Farmer's Tax Guide; Exemptions; Tax Withholding and Estimated Tax; Record-keeping for a Small Business; Self-employment Tax;* and literally dozens of others.

In particular, one important publication is IRS publication No. 587, *Business Use of Your Home.* It outlines the use requirements, exceptions and rules governing deductions, how to divide expenses, and which are deductible. It also provides a sample worksheet that reinforces the IRS message by encouraging you to practice. This publication is easy to read and helpful. It should be in your file on Home Business Management. For a copy, write to the Superintendent of Documents, U.S. Government Printing Office, Washington, DC 20402, Stock No. 048-004-01642-7.

Depreciation is described in IRS publication No. 534, and a *Tax Guide for Small Business* is described in publication No. 334. SBA publication 115B lists other SBA booklets that are easily available but which will cost you a little bit, in the $1-$5 range. Titles include, *Handbook of Small Business Finance; Profitable Community Relations for Small Business; Selecting Advertising Media—A Guide for Small Business,* and *Strengthening Small Business Management.* These are only a few of the listed publications.

Try to take advantage of these government resources. They have been set up to aid and assist people who want to act on ideas, and who are motivated to turn them into profitable business concerns.

CHECKLISTS FOR HOME BUSINESS OWNERS

Starting Expenses

(1) Permits & Licenses

(2) Equipment

(3) Inventory

(4) Advertising

(5) Legal & Professional Fees

(6) Professional-looking Stationery

Legal/Regulatory

(1) Register Business Name

(2) City and Zoning Laws

(3) Resale Permit

(4) Licenses

(5) State Tax

(6) Self-Employment Tax

(7) Knowing that you are operating "Within the Law"

If You Hire Employees:

(1) Social Security

(2) Workmen's Compensation

(3) Employee I.D.

(4) Insurance

(5) Federal Withholding Tax

Marketing

(1) Research Your Market

(2) Know Your Competition

(3) Structure Prices

(4) Advertising

(5) Publicity Campaign

(6) Sales Objectives

(7) Overall Marketing Budget & Plan

Financial

(1) Startup Needs

(2) Profit Projections

(3) Know Your Fixed Expenses

(4) Tax Plan

(5) Investment Plan

Five Mistakes to Avoid

(1) Poor Planning

(2) Poor Management

(3) Misuse of Time

(4) Bad Record-keeping

(5) Lack of Persistence

SECTION TWO:

Profitable Home Business Opportunities

In this section I am going to present you with approximately 100 different ways people are making money with their own home businesses. The opportunity, or opportunities (there is nothing wrong with starting more than one venture at a time, as long as you are willing to spend the time and make the effort) that are right for you, could be here.

The best home business for you should not only offer great monetary rewards, but also be a venture that is in tune with your unique personality. Over the years I have discovered that people excel when they are involved in activities that they genuinely enjoy. Making money is a motivational factor, but it definitely is **not** the only one.

Read on and reap the rewards...

GRASS ROOTS CAPITALISM—

SUCCESSFUL GARAGE SALES

The reader of my *Stay Home and Make Money* manual may be wondering why this information on garage sales has been included. The reader may be thinking, "Everyone knows about garage sales—how to attend one or hold one." While the basics of garage sales or lawn sales may be pretty much general knowledge, it is my intention to give you specific information that can make your next sale the biggest, best, most enjoyable and most profitable ever. A successful garage sale can be an excellent method to raise capital for other ventures.

The truly successful garage sale requires careful planning, with the important factors given thoughtful consideration. One of the best methods to use in preparing for a successful garage or lawn sale is to first attend many others and evaluate each one of them. Which kind of garage sales appear to be the most popular? What items seem to sell best? Which method of displaying items appears to be best? Etcetera, etcetera.

DECIDE WHAT YOU WILL SELL

Begin by looking over all your belongings. Decide which items you couldn't live without and which ones you could

37

live better without. Making decisions on just what you want to sell is step number one. Take an hour or two to go through every part of your house and garage to list your "potential sale inventory." You don't have to make a final decision yet. If you're like most of us, you will discover hundreds of items you did not even know you had. Nevertheless, once found, you will doubt whether to include these newly-found treasures in your sale. That's okay. You're just making a thorough list of your belongings (a good thing to do occasionally, even when not planning a garage sale). Later you will decide what to sell and what to keep.

WHAT ITEMS CAN BE SOLD
AT A GARAGE SALE?

The answer to that questions is easy...almost anything! Following is a list (only partial, believe me) of items I have noticed recently at garage sales here in Southern California (and I'm sure similar goods are being offered in all areas of the nation and the world).

Books	Bolts of material
Bookcases	Linens
Clothing	Coffee tables
Small appliances	Clothes hampers
Buffet	Dining tables
Dishes	End tables
Bicycles	Golf clubs
Mag wheels	Pots & pans
Gardening tools	Lamps
Candy	Picture frames
Eggs	Car parts
Fruit	Pool tables
Vegetables	Ping pong tables
Life preservers	Electronic components
Rocking chairs	Electric motors
Suitcases	Scuba gear
Christmas ornaments	Electric trains
Baskets	Slide rules

Porch swing
Cameras
Tapedeck
Chainsaw
Ice chests
Light fixture
Card tables
Pocket calculators
Drafting table
Hat racks
Avon bottles
Picture frames
Toaster ovens
Swing sets
Computer
Tents
Macrame
Quilts
Stuffed animals
Depression glass
Campers
Clay pots
Stove
Screen wire
Inner tubes
Ice cream freezer
Fishing gear
Art supplies
Vacuum cleaner
Antiques
Rugs
Stove venting hood
Telescope
Patio furniture
Exerciser bike
Blenders
Post cards
Posters
Fireplace equipment
Old bottles
Dishwasher

Rollaway beds
Smoke detectors
Barstools
Flatware
Workbench
Stained glass
Candle sticks
Basketballs
Back pack
Filing cabinet
Dehumidifier
Croquet sets
Stationery items
Fence wire
Tools
Record players
Radios
TV sets
Kitchen utensils
Wooden chairs
Baby beds
Children's clothing
Canoes
House plants
Games
Saws
Steam irons
Electric drills
Aquarium
Wooden shutters
Knives and guns
Lawnmower
Saddle
Books
Wheelbarrow
Tires
Canning jars
Loveseats/chairs
Old casement windows
Decorative pillows
Director chairs

Handcrafted items
Mixers
Knicknacks
Playpens
Costume jewelry
Coffee pots
Pottery
Skis
Room-size heaters
Roller skates
Pianos
Jigsaw puzzles
Venetian blinds
Bedspreads
Doll houses
Hedge trimmers
Collectible beer cans
Puppies and kittens
Ironing boards
Sinks
Used lumber
Typewriters
Fans
Air conditioners
Drums

Car parts
Cameras
Dressers
Sporting equipment
Alarm clocks
Magazines
Cedar chest
Sewing machines
Window screens
Dog houses
Mattresses
Mirrors
Drapes and rods
Silverware
Lithographs
Rope
Fiddles
Guitars
Grandfather clock
Table saw
Ladders
Desks
Cassette tapes
Record albums
Produce

PLAN FOR SUCCESS

A profitable garage sale is a well-planned garage sale. To run a successful sale, you should think of your garage sale as a business—a venture that requires little or no startup capital but one that richly rewards creative merchandising—displaying every item to its best advantage—and above all, creative thinking!

If you have ever held a garage sale or even just attended one, you probably already know some of the basic things that must be attended to concerning setup, display and pricing.

It is easy to let things slide till the last minute, but when you do, there is confusion as customers arrive while you're still trying to get your goods organized. Such a sale, even if it does earn a tidy profit, does much less than it could have if basic planning had been carried out.

DISPLAY AND LABELING

How items are displayed and labeled is essential to the success of a garage sale.

Price-labeling (you will find a selection of various sized labels at any stationery store) merchandise helps customers and forces you to make price decisions before the first customer shows up. Don't use supermarket prices such as 99¢, $1.98, etc. The same folks who accept those prices at their favorite market will resent them at a garage sale. Keep it simple: 50¢, $1, $1.50, $2, etc. Also remember—the more change items (10¢, 25¢, 50¢, $1.50, etc.) you have, the more additional change you will have to have in your pocket to make change. A metal box is often helpful to hold several dollars worth of nickels, dimes and quarters as well as dollar bills, fives and tens. This author has seen sales lost at a garage sale when a gentleman tried to buy a three dollar item with a twenty dollar bill. The nice lady running the sale could not cash the bill, and the man shook his head in annoyance and drove off. Be prepared. Keep plenty of change—bills and coins—on hand.

Although I strongly recommend price-labeling all your goods, I am not telling you not to negotiate. Price-haggling is an intimate part of flea markets, swap meets and garage sales, and in the case of negotiations, the price sticker on the item can act as a starting point.

I think it is wise to label all small price items (under two dollars) at the exact price you want for them and to hold to your cheaper prices. On items over two dollars, I recommend "marking them up" by 10% to 20% to give you plenty of room for negotiations.

After labeling all your merchandise, display it to each item's best advantage. Don't just heap one item on top of another in unsightly "piles." Think of yourself as a "department store" owner or the proprietor of a "variety store" and merchandise like they do. Show your goods off to their best advantage. Use household throw rugs, colorful sheets, blankets, etc., to act as an attractive backdrop to your merchandise. Card tables, folding tables and a chest of drawers (even if it is not included in the sale items) can help display items. If the garage is overcrowded, get some of your goods out on the driveway or lawn. (Caution: some shoplifting has occurred at garage sales. If you're having a particularly big sale, have your wife, kids or a friend assist you. Also, keep the most expensive items in plain view at all times.)

Cardboard boxes are great for displaying many items (books, records, small toys, novelties, etc.), but use your boxes only for items suited to them. Cramming boxes with clothing, for example, is not effective. The best way to display clothing for top prices and maximum sales is to set up a metal rod or clothesline from one side of the garage to another (or on poles outdoors) and use hangers for each clothing item.

CLEANLINESS BRINGS MORE CASH

Since many items sold at yard and garage sales have seen little or no recent use, a lot of it is dirty. Most of the folks who attend these weekend sales expect to find items covered with dust and dirt. You can earn more money by surprising them! A bucket of soapy water and a couple of old rags can have most items looking spic and spiffy in no time. Experience has taught me that clean merchandise will outsell dusty or dirty goods—and at a much higher price. Keep in mind that on Sundays many of the people coming to your sale will be doing so before or after attending church. These people will be well-dressed and are reluctant to handle any item that is not squeaky clean.

OTHER ITEMS TO HAVE AVAILABLE

☐ Change: As mentioned earlier, you do not want to lose sales because you cannot make proper change. One roll each of nickels, dimes and quarters (a total of $17) plus one ten dollar bill, two fives and twenty ones would be a minimum amount for an average garage sale. A total of $57.

☐ Tape measure: Folks often will ask how long or wide an item is (especially furniture), and it will help you make a sale to give them exact dimensions.

☐ Electrical outlet and extension cord: People shy away from buying radios, TVs, recorders, lamps, etc., that they have no way of knowing if they are in proper running condition. Put their fears to rest and you probably can make the sale.

☐ Paper bags, boxes, old newspapers, wrapping paper, string, etc. It is good business to make it easy for people to haul away the goods.

ADVERTISING

The single most common reason why many garage sales flop is inadequate promotion and advertising.

Almost everyone who puts on a garage sale does some advertising—perhaps a small listing in the paper or at least a handmade sign down on a corner telephone pole. *This is not enough!* If you are after maximum profits, you increase—rather than decrease—advertising. Additional advertising can and will greatly increase your traffic flow; and as with any other small business, increased traffic flow means increased sales!

SIGNS: Keep them simple but effective. Don't skimp. Maybe you could get by with one or two signs at the nearest intersection, but you don't want to just get by. You're after heavy traffic. If it takes six signs strategically placed—prepare six signs. Any and all intersections within a three-block radius should be covered, even if that means ten signs! Your only investment in signs should be a marking pen. A cardboard box cut up will yield two to four signs, depending on size. Even brown grocery bags will be fine, unless it's a windy day.

Keep your signs easy to read. Don't scribble a whole lot of details on your paper or cardboard. Handprint neatly with big black letters—GARAGE SALE—and put an arrow under that. No more. No less. Keep in mind—cars tooling along at thirty miles per hour or more are moving too fast for their drivers to see anything more than a few large words.

Some people can't even write GARAGE SALE in big, neat, easy-to-read letters. These folks should turn the signmaking chores over to a spouse or friend.

NEWSPAPER ADS

Find which paper in your area carries the most garage sale ads and jump in with them. Don't waste your money in small papers that carry little or no garage sale ads. Don't worry if you live in a big city that has a daily paper with hundreds of other garage sale ads in it. People tend to go to those sales that are within a few miles from where they live. If they live near you, they'll come to your sale, not one across town.

Classified ads will end up paying handsome dividends. Newspapers usually charge by the line or by the word. Guess what happens? 95% of all people hold expenses to a minimum with a tiny ad. Here's an example of a tiny garage sale classified newspaper ad:

Garage sale. Many different items.
Sat. and Sun. 1063 Midway Drive

44

Not too exciting, is it? About as exciting as warm milk and crackers. Now look at this ad:

Gigantic Garage Sale, Sunday Only!
100s of items—TV, radios, waterbed,
dining room table, coin collection, books,
records, much more! 770 Seacliff Dr.

Sure, the first ad may have cost a couple of dollars less than the second; however, the bigger ad will stand out and bring double or triple the response. To be successful, you must stand out from the pack. A large classified ad is one sure method to get your sale increased attention. A bigger ad gives the impression you have a bigger sale. Folks love to go where there is an abundance of merchandise to dig through.

Another tip regarding ads: If you live on a street that is not easily recognizable, give your address but also mention a well-known nearby street, such as:

103 Sun St., 1 block east of Main St.

HOW TO ENTICE CUSTOMERS
TO GET OUT OF THEIR CARS
AND WALK UP TO YOUR GARAGE SALE

Your signs and ads, if you have followed the advice given, will get many people to drive up to your place. Some will be driving slowly and looking; most will stop and look. Only after this "look-see" will they decide whether to park and pay you a personal visit.

If your sale is not at least somewhat visible from the street you could have many folks drive off rather than hunt for you. If your house and garage is not readily visible, you must use several additional signs that point the way. If, for example, you live in a large apartment complex and are holding your garage sale in your individual carport, you better offer a series of easy-to-read signs leading folks to your exact location.

If your selling area is highly visible from the street, so much the better. This allows you the opportunity to entice your would-be customers with some promotional gimmicks. Give your sale all the "drawing power" you possibly can. Set up early and walk up to the street to see how appealing it looks. Have as much merchandise visible as possible. Color-coordinate clothing and other objects and have some things laid out, others hanging, etc., to create maximum appeal from the roadside looker.

SELLING TIPS

If you're not used to selling things one-to-one to other people, these tips may help you relate well to your potential buyers:

☐ Smile and say "hello" to everyone who comes by.

☐ Allow people to browse on their own until they ask you for help. If you start asking them questions about what they are looking for, they'll probably say "just looking." If you persist, they may feel uncomfortable and leave.

☐ Keep an eye on your most valuable merchandise—especially small items like jewelry—but don't make this too obvious. No one likes to feel they are being watched closely.

☐ Once a customer offers you a price lower than the price marked on an object, be ready to enter into "friendly negotiations." If all your expensive items are priced exactly 20% above the lowest price you will accept (and it pays you to consider this pricing method before the sale starts), it will be easy for you to negotiate.

Here's a typical negotiating exchange and how you may wish to handle it:

46

Customer: "Will you take seven dollars for this lamp?"

Seller (after noting that he has priced it at ten dollars): "I priced it at ten dollars, and I thought that was very cheap."

Customer: "Well, how much do you want for it?"

Seller: "I would like to get ten dollars."

Customer: "How about eight?"

Seller: "How about nine dollars? That would be a good buy."

Customer: "I'll give you eight dollars and fifty cents."

Seller: "All right. You're certainly a good negotiator."

Another important point regarding price: Don't offer items for sale (especially possible antique treasures or art items) by guessing at their price. You may make a mistake and price them too high, and they won't sell, or you might make an even bigger mistake and sell them for too little. When in doubt, do not offer for sale. Have all rare or possible antique items appraised.

HOW MUCH MONEY WILL YOUR SALE BRING?

This is a highly subjective question. The more items you offer for sale, the bigger your total cash receipts (which reminds me, garage sale selling is a cash business—no checks, except from friends).

The amount of money the average garage sale brings in is usually slightly under seventy-five dollars for one day or under one hundred twenty-five for two days. Using the techniques and tactics mentioned in this chapter, you can do twice or three times this amount.

We know a Van Nuys, California couple who hold a garage sale once every four or five weeks (when not holding their own sale, they are attending other sales and buying items they later mark up) and seldom take in less than three hundred dollars for a one-day sale!

Garage sales, for some, are a once a year method to earn some nice money while getting rid of unwanted items. For others, they are a part-time home business.

MAKING MONEY AT FLEA MARKETS AND SWAP MEETS

Much of what has been discussed concerning successful garage sales also applies to selling at flea markets and swap meets. Make your goods look good and do everything to draw people to your selling area.

With thousands of flea markets and swap meets now operating all over the United States, and the world, these weekly "events" (while many are staged only on weekends, several of the larger ones operate all week long, or at least 3 or 4 days or nights per week) have become great places to make substantial money.

At many of these outdoor or indoor selling extravaganzas, used (garage sale-type) items account for part of the goods being sold, while unique *homemade* items and new general merchandise bought wholesale for resale, are also found in abundance.

Ten years ago I was involved in buying and reselling sunglasses from several Oriental countries (Taiwan, Japan, and Korea). The original plan was to market these sunglasses to retailers (drugstores, liquor stores, etc.), which we did. Soon, however, we realized there was real money to be made in making sales at major swap meets in San Diego, and the nearby communities of El Cajon, Escondido, Spring Valley, and National City. I was skeptical concerning how much money could be made at these open-air marketplaces. A friend, Frank Davis, who was selling at these meets, convinced me there was money to be made. How right he was! Our first Sunday at the swap meet at San Diego Stadium was a revelation. We sold one thousand dollars worth of sunglasses in one day. Net profit: approximately $650. Soon, we hired others to work for us on a commission basis, and our sunglasses and other items (hats, visors, belt buckles, novelty items, etc.) were prominently displayed and sold at all leading meets in the county. (For reasons unknown to me, many of these great open-air marketplaces are called swap meets in the Western states, while being labeled flea markets in most Midwestern and Eastern states.)

Rental space is usually very inexpensive, $8.00 and up per day, determined by the size of the space you rent, and the crowd flows each market produces.

While some sharp, buy low-sell high dealers are making good profits with used merchandise, the majority of sharp operators who are cashing in big (and profits in the $500 to $5,000 range per week are not unusual) are selling new merchandise.

Any craft items that you can make inexpensively are a good candidate for flea market or swap meets sales, as are food stuffs that you grow or cook.

For most, the profits are made in buying items for resale. The key to success is attractive, impulse merchandise, at attractive prices.

You don't want to be selling the same items available at Sears or K-Mart, unless your price is less. In addition to buying on impulse, the folks who frequent these marketplaces—and millions do nationwide—are looking for bargains. Closeout merchandise can bring a windfall of profits. Check out the Sunday editions of large, metropolitan newspapers for such buy-outs. Also you may wish to contact importers, searching for unique new items.

Following is a group of firms that offer information on a wide variety of attractive, low-priced merchandise at big discount prices. Get on the mailing list of all these concerns if you wish to consider swap meet/flea market selling.

The Sutton Family
11565 Ridgewood Circle, N.
Seminole, FL 33542

Edens
246 Main St.
Monson, MA 01057

write each and ask what they charge for placement on their mailing list

Specialties International
Box 862
Clute, TX 77531

Pioneer Trading Co.
3922 W. Irving Park Rd.
Chicago, IL 60618

Marco Novelty Co.
Box 705
Ashburn, GA 31714

Galaxy Electronics
5300 21st Ave.
Brooklyn, NY 11204

World Distributors
3311 W. Montrose Ave.
Chicago, IL 60616

Hetrick Products
1656 Hagey Dr.
Barberton, OH 44203

Advance Distributors
4949 N. Pulaski
Chicago, IL 60630

Capital City
484 Central Ave.
Albany, NY 12206

R. O'Donnell
9 Sewanois Ave.
Lincoln Park, NJ 07035

National Flea Marketeer
11565 Ridgewood Circle, N.
Seminole, FL 33542

DRAW CUSTOMERS TO YOUR BOOTH

With hundreds of sellers at the big flea markets and meets, you must get the attention of all those valuable shoppers. You must stand out! Don't junk up your booth or space with messy signs or an overall sloppy appearance. Design attractive day-glow signs with your sale slogans and specials. If you don't print very clearly, get someone that does to help. Set up tables (the folding variety work well here) and display your goods attractively. A canopy not only can protect you from sun or rain, if you're outside, but also gives you a professional appearance.

I have discovered the most successful dealers are the ones who operate in the same way as a successful small store or boutique. You may have to "fold up your tent" and go home each day, but to be successful, run it just like a full-fledged business, which it is!

CASHING IN ON YOUR BRIGHT IDEAS AND CREATIVE INVENTIONS

On the following pages I am going to give you examples of the power of positive and creative thinking combined with positive action. A fortune awaits the home inventor who has "the right idea!"

The man or woman with good ideas and the willingness to put them into action will always prosper in this world.

Creativity alone is not enough. Undisciplined creative thinking is nothing more than a mind exercise. Financial rewards are achieved when creative thinking is combined with CAN-DO thinking, followed by decisive action, the "tremendous trio" of real success.

All moneymaking endeavors and inventions must begin with a creative idea, but creative action must sooner or later come into partnership with the bright thought if monetary rewards are to be obtained.

Creative ideas, including ideas that can make you a fortune, are found in your subconscious mind. The best way to unlock the key to your subconcious is to learn the techniques of *Mental Science* and creative thinking. Many, many people from all over the world have told me that my

53

442-page book, *How to Achieve Total Success*, has helped them *unlock the secret door* to their subconscious mind, and bring forth a steady stream of powerful new ideas. I think you will greatly benefit by reading this book.

ASK YOURSELF QUESTIONS

Your success can depend on your ability to ask the right questions of yourself and your brainchild. Even if you have a knowledgeable background in the field you are drawing your creation from, there is room for creative questions.

Does it really work?
Is it really new?
Is it economical?
Is it practical?
Is it desirable?
And the most important question of all—
Who will buy it?

It behooves you to come up with thoughtful answers to every conceivable and reasonable question pertaining to your invention. Do you invent for personal satisfaction only, or are you thinking about potential markets?

KNOW WHAT TO INVENT

While almost everybody of sound mind is capable of inventing something (we all are unconsciously creating events and circumstances in our lives daily), only a small percentage of us seem to know what to consciously invent.

The majority of inventors of new products and gadgets seem to be somewhat impractical in their inventions. A case

---

How to Achieve Total Success by Russ von Hoelscher, © 1983, 1987, Profit Ideas.

in point: TV star Johnny Carson recently invited a California man on his popular "Tonight Show." This guy had been inventing crazy, impractical stuff for twenty years. One of his brainchildren was a huge mechanical monster, put together by a ton of scrap iron, with the sole purpose of swatting a fly, should one ever land on its front plate. When Johnny inquired how long it took to build this monstrosity and how much it would cost, the inventor answered nine months and ten thousand dollars, respectively. While it is possible some eccentric may pay ten grand for this jewel, most of us will continue to buy the ordinary 49¢ fly swatter at the supermarket or hardware store.

My point in all this is to emphasize it isn't good business to invent something strange and then seek a market. First seek out a potential market and then invent something practical or strange.

MAKING MONEY THROUGH SALE
OR LICENSE

The people who usually earn the biggest profits are those who both invent and market (or even market others' creations). However, if you're short on marketing capital and do not want to hunt for partners, or for any other reasons do not want to found a business or expand your present business, the alternative is to sell your patent or give someone else a license to use it. Obviously, to be in the best bargaining position, you should get your patent before you look to sell or license the thing. Legally, until you have been given a patent by the government, you can't stop anyone from using your invention.

Once you decide to license or sell your invention, don't make one proposal to one prospective buyer and leave it go at that. Put in enough time to develop a list of potential buyers and get busy via personal contact, the phone and the mail to "allow them to make an offer on your revolutionary new creation." Personal contact is best! But if you're in

Tucson, Arizona and your list of companies to contact includes several in New York and Chicago, the mail and telephone will usually have to do.

Just remember, "Selling is the key factor..." Make every remotely possible use of your product or gadget known to a potential buyer or licensee.

Keep in mind an "exclusive license" is the same as an outright sale for the period of time in the contract; and if a firm asks for a long "exclusive" (and anything over two years can be l-o-n-g in the marketing business), you should ask for almost as much as you would if you sold all rights unconditionally.

HOW TO FIND SOMEONE TO MARKET YOUR IDEA OR INVENTION

Many "idea people" find the process of creating and inventing more stimulating and enjoyable than distribution, marketing and sales; however, most creative people make great marketing and sales people, if they put themselves to the task. This is important because if the creative person decides to sell or license his offspring, he will have a better shot at success if he understands something about marketing strategy.

Let's suppose your new invention is an economical device that makes "instant ice cream" from the basic ingredients (vanilla, cream, sugar, salt, etc.). You believe you have a red-hot item that millions of consumers will be craving to buy. You have applied for a patent through a patent attorney, and your claims have all been granted, but the patent has not been issued yet. A typical situation. Now we shall try to select a company that is able to market our great new ice cream sensation that we call simply "Instant Ice Cream Maker." What kind of firm should we pick? A new company? An established corporation? One that sells housewares? One that distributes gadgets? Following is our marketing opinion based on this hypothetical product:

56

☐ Choose a manufacturer with many years of experience in housewares.

☐ Only an experienced manufacturer of housewares could judge this product's worth and have the volume of sales necessary to produce it at a mass-market price.

☐ An established firm with a line of products aimed at houseware buyers, even if none of their other products are related to your invention, can spread the cost of its sales force over its entire product lineup. In this way, the product line can help carry a new addition until it, hopefully, takes off!

WHO TO TALK TO

The size, internal positions and worth of each company dictates the degree of formality required in the submission procedure. Even a small firm may ask you to sign a release (you should do this when requested) not to sue them for examining your gadget. This is usually mandatory with big companies. You're protected by the patent, so don't worry about this.

With small companies, the president himself (or herself) may make the ultimate decision on whether to add your invention to their line. With the major concerns, the concept will first have to pass inspection by the people in charge of the "New Products" Department or the Research and Development Lab.

The good folks in R&D or New Products probably won't have the final say on the manufacture and sale of your invention, but their favorable comments will go a long way in convincing the powers-that-be in the company to give your gadget the "green light." Likewise, no interest shown in R&D will probably kill any potential deal.

If you don't like wasting precious time, make sure you are

making your initial critical presentation to the right person or persons.

TURN REJECTION INTO ACCEPTANCE

Probably the most important step in learning how to market inventions is to keep your project moving forward. You can expect delays, communication breakdowns and rejections. Just don't let these negative aspects bring your project to a halt, provided that you have absolute confidence in your creation that is backed by logic.

You must be logical in evaluating a turndown. Don't fall in love with your project to the degree that you close your ears and mind to a "logical rejection." When a knowledge-able production engineer, research and development person or marketing expert explains to you that your brainchild is not going to work well or sell well—he just might be right! Never abandon your pet project on only one man's opinion. Seek out all the expert advice available. Look at your gismo from all sides and up and down. Perhaps you can find one key element that can transform it from a "no sale" to full acceptance and success!

Never abandon a project on the say-so of one or two others, even if they are considered very competent in this field. However, if you do run out of ways to improve your gizmo, and just about every expert you ask an opinion of sees no future in your invention, it is probably time to move on to another project. Why waste time with something that holds little promise? You're creative! You can invent something that will be a hit!!

HOW TO GO INTO BUSINESS
WITH YOUR INVENTION

Marketing ideas and inventions is a business, and while super success is possible, this enterprise is not without pitfalls.

58

Let's return to work with our hypothetical "Instant Ice Cream" invention. If we decided to go into business marketing this new invention instead of selling the rights to another to do the manufacturing and promotion, several steps would be required.

A. We would need to find a tool and die company to cast the original die.

B. Once we had the prototype, we would need to solicit bids from several machine shops regarding production and choose someone to produce the gadget, unless we intend to establish a manufacturing facility (a very big project that could be very expensive).

C. A distribution and marketing plan would have to be implemented (if we are smart we had a marketing plan in mind *before* any other phase went into action).

D. Our company would have to launch a publicity campaign.

E. Our company would have to launch an advertising campaign.

F. Shipping and receiving departments and warehousing would need to be set up.

G. A mail-handling clerical and billing department would be called for.

H. Bookkeeping, filing and other supportive systems would have to be implemented.

All of the above functions (but not necessarily in the order given) plus a hundred and one other duties and details would be associated with the manufacture of our new invention. If we're starting on a shoestring budget, most of these business responsibilities will fall on our wife's or our drooping shoulders. Nobody said it would be easy! If we're of the true creative entrepreneur bent, a few obstacles (or even a few hundred) won't stop us!

While I do admire the man who launches his own business, starting with his own invention, the outlook for success in this type of business is dubious. Lacking either enough expertise or enough capital in the inventing/manufacturing/sales business can make this a risky venture.

GETTING STARTED RIGHT

If you decide to "go for it" and establish your own firm, there are specific processes of handling a new invention.

The two pillars of potential success in marketing your own creation are:

(1) Manufacturing

(2) Sales

While common sense may tell us that we need to materialize (manufacture) our hot new invention before we can sell it, good business tactics demand that we place our strongest emphasis on our sales technique. Sales will be the factor that makes us or breaks us!

Since many businesses are established without sufficient funds to set up both manufacturing and sales facilities simultaneously, it probably would be in our best interest to put most of our limited capital on getting our invention sold. You can use a good machine shop's (get competitive bids from several) injection molders and other needed supplies.

As for kicking off your sales campaign, many a new enterprise has started with a few samples hand-manufactured in somebody's garage, a collection of photographs and some well-written instructions and sales literature.

GET SOME EXPERT HELP

A good accountant—one who has some experience working with start-up ventures—and a business attorney can give you needed advice. A manufacturing and sales consultant could also provide expert opinion.

If you need more capital than you have, you will have to contact a cash-lending source. These can range from friends and relatives to your banker. Friends and relatives usually require less interest and can be a great source for a "cheap loan." The big problem here is if your hot invention turns ice cold and your business goes "belly up," you could find yourself with friends who are no more or relatives who are not speaking to you. You won't have this problem with banks, but unless you have a strong line of credit, you probably will have to put up plenty of collateral to be able to rent their money. Perhaps your best source of money would be "risk capital" from a private source. You could easily pay such a source twice as much interest as you would an established financial institution, but anyone who is willing to gamble their money on a new invention probably deserves a high return on investment.

A well-worded ad in a large circulation daily newspaper could bring you the source of needed capital. Sometimes these investors will work with you strictly for a return on investment; at other times they may demand a percentage of your business—in other words, a limited partnership. While you may desire only a loan, there are times when accepting a silent or limited partner could be beneficial or even the only method available to get your new business venture going.

HOW TO PROTECT YOUR INVENTIONS

Get the facts concerning a patent. Using a patent attorney is advisable. Patent offices move, fees go up, laws change, etc. A patent attorney can provide current facts.

If you're doing your own filing, you can send your Record of Invention to the Patent Office, in duplicate, and they will date both copies officially. Then, they will keep one copy and return the other to you. Why two copies? Because they will keep this record for only two years. If you apply for a patent, it will be added to the application, but, if not, their copy will be destroyed.

It is often necessary to delay (mostly to improve) your application for a patent, so having your own copy of the date of your ideas, which cannot be questioned, is a far better proof than the older method. To learn the details, send for the free booklet entitled: Disclosure Document Program to: The U.S. Department of Commerce, Patent Office, Washington, D.C. 20231.

To prepare an acceptable Record of Invention properly use a good-quality white paper of a size not to exceed 8½x13" (regular 8½x11" letter size is acceptable), and type a brief, lucid explanation of your invention (not personal details as to where and how you got the inspiration).

Describe the structure; its function; its intended uses and its essential differences from existing related devices. If the invention can be illustrated in drawings, use letters or numbers on those drawings to denote important points or areas, and use those references in your written explanation. If you must write by hand, use ink, not pencil, for pencil smudges with the years and can be erased and changed long after the sketches were made; hence, it is not legal. Sign and date your disclosure; have two witnesses read and sign it too. For a duplicate, have a clear photocopy made of your Record of Invention, and for safety, have two made up (one to keep until the dated record is returned). Then, send the original and one copy to: Commissioner of Patents, U.S. Patent Office, Washington, D.C. 20231, together with a $10 check or money order (do not send cash) made out to the Commissioner of Patents. If more than one page of disclosure is necessary, number each page thus: page 1 of two pages (or three), and sign and date each page at the bottom. Now, send the two copies with a self-addressed envelope, properly stamped, for their return of your duplicate copy. Attach a separate note reading:

The undersigned, being the inventor of the disclosed invention, requests that the enclosed papers be accepted under the Disclosed Document Program, and that they be preserved for a period of two years. Please stamp-date and return the duplicate copy.

HOW TO PROTECT YOUR IDEAS

Ideas can be protected, not in their abstract form but in certain "projected physical form." There are many forms of protection for creative people that our government offers. Here is a brief resume of the type of protection available.

• For artistic designs of clothes, furniture, automobiles, furniture, etc., there is the design patent.

• For invention of mechanical, chemical and electrical products and devices, there is the United States patent.

• For original, asecually produced plants...the plant patent.

• For artistic things such as poems, songs, novels, factual writings, cartoons, etc...the copyright.

• For trade names in actual use...the Trademark.

HOW TO SUBMIT AN IDEA
TO A COMPANY

Should you wish to submit an idea to a company for their evaluation, and if this idea has not yet been subject to a copyright or does not apply to an invention, etc., here is semi-official procedure used by many "idea people":

Once a bright idea enters your mind, jot it down or type it on a piece of paper.

Go into detail, elaborate upon it as much as possible. Then, pop your written sheet in an envelope and take it to your local Post Office. Via registered mail, have the envelope registered, postmarked and mailed to yourself. Do not open it! Put it in a safe place (with your other important papers) and hold it for possible future reference. While there is no federal statute that pertains to this procedure, a recent court decision in Iowa awarded several thousands of dollars to a man who produced a sealed, registered letter, which proved the company he was consulting with used his idea for streamlining their production plant without paying him one penny for his concept.

While this idea protection technique is not as iron-clad as a U.S. Patent, Trademark or Copyright, it is far better than no protection at all. Most firms who will entertain your ideas will not use them without offering you compensation, but why not give yourself a little extra insurance protection? This is what you get using the self-addressed, sealed, registered letter.

HOW TO MAKE MONEY AS A FREE-LANCE CONSULTANT

Most people who work for someone else will never make big money. If you give your company brilliant ideas on how to increase profits by many thousands of dollars, you'll probably get a pat on the back. If you're lucky, you might get a raise. If, however, you're my kind of gal or guy, a *mover, shaker and moneymaker,* you'll present your great business-building plans, in the role of a consultant. A sharp consultant may like an ego-pleasing pat on the back—that's better than a kick in the pants—but what he or she really wants is the money, baby.

Almost every business owner is looking for ways to make more money. Borderline businesses need to find ways to increase productivity and profits, or they will decline and eventually fail. Businesses that are already showing nice bottom line black ink are seldom satisfied. They want to make more money. Sound familiar?

If you have expertise in any specific area of business or management, consulting could be for you. In fact, there is a whole range of activities, in which business is only one of the primary ones, that employ free-lance consultants.

If you have knowledge in a field, and *specialized knowledge* is the key to success, and there is a market willing to pay for it, you could be making money as a home-based consultant.

I have always believed in helping people by teaching them what I know. One major reason the *Fast Start* book dealers program has become so successful is because I offer phone consulting to all of my dealers. However, as my workload increased, I found that increased demands on my time required new approaches to helping people. While my time, via the telephone, will always be available to those who actively sell our books and tapes, I now also stage mail order success seminars and self-publishing/book-selling workshops on a regular basis. When a company or individual requires my service on a one-to-one basis, my consulting fee is currently $100 an hour (minimum of two hours) or $650 for one full day.

Knowledge that can help another make money, save time, or in any way make a person's life more fulfilling is a saleable commodity. The way people make money in consulting is to have specialized information that others desire.

Here are just a few of the countless ways people are making money in consulting:

Advertising
Business Acquisition
Business Management
Closet and Space Organization
Copywriting
Data Management
Direct Mail
Direct Selling
Environment Advisor
Farm Management
Fashion Coordinator
Food Services
Graphic Arts
Home or Office Organization
Interior Design Planning
Publicist

...and the list goes on and on.

If you have valuable information on almost any topic, there is a way to sell your knowledge as an independent consultant.

Two highly recommended books on the subject are:

How to Succeed as an Independent Consultant, by Herman Holtz. John Wiley & Sons, Inc., New York, New York.

The Consultant's Kit, by Dr. Jeffrey Lant. JLA Publications, Cambridge, Massachusetts.

(Ordering instructions for both these books can be found in the Resource Directory in this book.)

FINDING CUSTOMERS FOR
YOUR CONSULTING PRACTICE

While less than adequate *capitalization* is the cause of failure for several new business ventures, this is seldom the reason a consultant fails. You can get started in this lucrative business on the proverbial shoestring. But you must be *market smart*!

Gathering leads and turning them into new customers is the key to success for any new consultant. In other words, effective marketing! Sell yourself! Sell your practice!

Where is your market? How do you identify those companies or individuals who need—and are willing to pay for—your professional services?

If companies make up the major portion of your potential consulting marketplace, you must reach them initially in one of three ways: (1) in person, (2) by telephone, or (3) by mail. Obviously, you may choose to use all three methods.

Here's an example: For many years, Red Reiss, of Pasadena, California, managed the shipping and receiving department for a large paper company. He learned and developed several innovative ways to maximize warehouse space and efficiently handle his firm's shipping and receiving operation. When Red decided to offer his knowledge to other companies, he used personal contact, the phone and the mail to get in touch with various mid-size to large industrial companies throughout Southern California; he outlined (but did not fully explain) his innovative methods in his conversations and mailing brochures. Since Red can completely revise and improve a company's warehouse and shipping/receiving department within about 30 days, he sells himself and his services to a company as an on-site consultant for one full month. Once he has completed this time on-site and has the warehouse and shipping operation running smoothly, he gives the company the option of retaining his services on a "twice-a-year checkup" basis. If the company agrees that they would like to have this ongoing service, he is put on retainer.

Here's an example of a consultant who works for individuals. Cathy Schmidt of Tacoma, Washington, is a room and closet organizer. She markets her services mostly to individuals, although some business offices have also used her services. When Cathy discovered a direct mail campaign to new homeowners and apartment-dwellers in the Seattle-Tacoma area was not producing much new business for her fledgling consulting business, she tried a new tactic that brought lots of business and a successful practice.

Cathy visited upscale home furnishing stores in her area. She got to know the managers and sales personnel at these stores and boutiques, and let them know she could provide a vital service to their customers who wanted to maximize their living and closet space. The stores and shops referred new business to her, and her consulting business soon tripled in both volume and profits.

In any time of independent consulting, it's important that you define your marketplace, and then creatively consider the most cost-effective methods of obtaining new business. How much to charge clients can be determined by the exclusiveness of your service, and what the market will bear, using the fee schedules of other consultants, (don't be afraid to call them and ask questions) who are offering similar services to yours. As business builds, your fees should also be increased.

While consultants who make their services available to business establishments usually command more money than those who work with individuals, a popular people-oriented practice often has a never-ending supply of new clients, which is the lifeblood of a successful consulting practice.

Watch your local newspaper for "help wanted" ads. Sometimes a company will advertise a full-time position in the field of your expertise. Often you can convince such a firm that you can fulfill their needs on an ongoing part-time basis. This saves them money in the long run and allows you to earn regular fees while still having free time to accept other consultant assignments.

MAKE MONEY WITH A MICROCOMPUTER

The computer revolution of the 1970s has delivered the computer explosion of the 1980s! It also has paved the way for a new, very lucrative cottage industry that should continue to be profitable for home business entrepreneurs into the 1990s.

In his book *The Third Wave*, author Alvin Toffler predicts that the electronic cottage may be the mom and pop business of the future. Increasing numbers of home-based entrepreneurs are making his prediction their reality. Here are just a few examples on how people are profiting.

Computer Services—to do accounting, taxes, financial planning, word processing, mailing lists, inventory, etc.

Selling Computer Hardware and Related Items—In 1982, over, 1.6 million microcomputers were sold, and the demand is rapidly rising! Printers and other add-on computer devices also experienced huge sale increases. Computers are the fastest growing segment of the American economy, and should continue to be throughout the 1980s.

Marketing Programs—The huge number of microcomputers generates a large need for programs (software) that provides the computer with the instruction necessary to perform a given task. This is probably the fastest grow-

70

ing segment of the computer industry.

Information, Please—Many people want knowledge about computers. This promotes a market for providing information in the form of computer camps, schools, courses, books, publications and workshops.

Providing Supplies—Supplies such as labels, forms, paper, disk cleaners, etc., are also an expanding market area.

Computer Repairs—The increasing number of computers has resulted in a skyrocketing demand for repair centers. Anyone who can repair these little electronic monsters will seldom, if ever, be unemployed.

The above represent just a few of the obvious ways the electronic cottage industry tycoon can prosper in this field. There are many, many others, all associated with a computer and man's desire to become quickly informed on almost anything.

SELECTING YOUR MICROCOMPUTER

First things first! Before you can profit with a small computer, you must own or lease one. Competition is heavy, and the ads can be confusing. What's a person to do? Get your hands on a good computer selection book. This subject is too detailed to be presented here, so I am listing a trio of excellent books on this important subject. Look (study) before you leap. No two microcomputers are alike. Buy or lease only when you know exactly what you will be getting. These books will help you make an informed decision.

COMPUTER SELECTION GUIDE—Choosing the Right Hardware and Software by Dan Poynter. The versatile and talented Mr. Poynter (he's also a publishing and aviation sports expert) has written another excellent book, this time on selecting your own computer. This book is basic and yet very complete, very easy-to-read, and understand. You'll be a very informed buyer after you read this excellent short course in selecting both hardware and software. The price: $11.95 plus $1.00 postage/handling from: PARA PUBLISHING, P.O. Box 4232, Santa Barbara, CA 93103.

COMPUTERS FOR SMALL BUSINESS—A Step-by-Step Guide on How to Buy by Gary Bencar is another great reference book and selection guide. Mr. Bencar owns his own computer consulting business and gives the reader, literally, several hundred dollars in expert advice for only $9.95 in this highly informative paperback manual. This book will teach you how to analyze your computer requirements, locate and evaluate the correct software, get the most value for your money, plus much more. Only $9.95 plus $1.00 postage/handling from LA CUMBRE PUBLISHING COMPANY, P.O. Box 30959, Santa Barbara, CA 93105.

CHOOSING A COMPUTER by Tom Alfred is another very useful guidebook. It is filled with problem-solving advice and valuable buyer-beware information. Unlike Poynter's or Bencar's books (both trade paperbacks), this offering comes in hardcover only. The price is $16.95 plus $2.00 postage/handling from NORTH STAR PRESS, P.O. Box 1324, North St. Paul, MN 55109.

Once you have wisely selected your new microcomputer, you are ready to provide the service of your choice. Here are some insights into what you may offer your customers:

PAYROLL SERVICE: A computerized payroll can save a company both time and money. Small firms (probably your most likely clients) of 5 to 50 employees can be expected to pay from 80¢ to $1.50 per employee per week for a payroll service. And many small business people will jump at the chance to get out from under the burden of preparing their own payroll.

ACCOUNTING: Accounting services are not as easy to set up and operate as a basic payroll service. Again, small to mid-size firms are your most likely customers. An individual program must be put in operation to fit the client's singular needs. Knowing computer hardware and software may not be enough to set up and maintain a sophisticated program. Going into business with an accountant could solve this problem.

One of the best sources of programs for computerized accounting is COMPUTRONICS, South Pascack Road, Spring Valley, NY 10977.

For assistance in charging for your computer services, write for current information on the valuable pricing manual, *CHARGING FOR COMPUTER SERVICES*, available from PBI BOOKS, 384 Fifth Avenue, New York, NY 10018.

Another excellent method to determine your fees is to query several competitors to discover the going rate in your area for professional services.

INCOME TAX PREPARATION: In addition to a good microcomputer, you'll need to complete a basic income tax preparation course, easily obtained through a local school or a correspondence school. There are a number of good software programs now on the market. You may write to these program headquarters for more details on software:

EZ TAX, 2444 Moorpark Rd., San Jose, CA 95128
MICRO TAX, P.O. Box 4262, Mountain View, CA 94040
OMEGA TAX SERVICE, 222 S. Riverside Plaza,
    Chicago, IL 60606
FEDERATED TAX, P.O. Box 1004, Port Huron, MI
    48060

MAILING LISTS: Many small publishers and active mail order firms must make regular mailings to their customers or subscribers. These firms need their mailing lists constantly updated—no easy task if done manually, but a snap for the correctly programmed microcomputer.

In this type of business you will face established

competition, but business is always available to the operator who is an aggressive sales person. Business can be obtained locally or through the use of mail order advertising or direct mail. Keep in mind, many companies are using direct mailings for at least part of their sales, including whole-salers, manufacturers and retailers.

Fees do vary. The range seems to be 5¢ to 10¢ per three- or four-line name and address for data entry and $10.00 to $20.00 per thousand name printout, depending on the label format.

You can write the following companies concerning mailing list programs:

PRECISION PROTOTYPES MAILING LISTS, 12221 Beaver Pike, Jackson, OH 45640

SOFTWARE CONCEPTS, 105 Preston Valley Shopping Center, Dallas, TX 75230

POWER SOFT, 11500 Stemmons Freeway, Dallas, TX 75229

COMPUTECH, 975 Forest Avenue, Lakewood, NY 08701

In addition to servicing and maintaining lists for others, profits are readily available for anyone who compiles their own lists for rental. Regardless of which type list you would compile—lawyers, doctors, accountants, teachers, students, etc., and the possibilities are endless—only offer to rent your names. This keeps customers placing repeat orders. Prices you can charge for list rentals can vary from $25.00 to $100.00 or more per 1,000 names, depending on the list and how easy or difficult it is to obtain.

A reliable and competitively priced source for all sorts of paper and mailing labels is MAIL ADVERTISING SUPPLY COMPANY, 1450 S. West Ave., Box 363, Waukesha, WI 53187.

PUBLISHING YOUR OWN SOFTWARE

A computer is only as good as the program that is given to it. The writing, production and marketing of software could make you very, very rich. Competition is fierce, but this is one arena where the individual can compete with the giant corporations. If you are creative and persevere, success can be yours.

You may have heard stories of people making a bundle through writing a computer program. A Minnetonka, Minnesota, man was recently paid $60,000 for a new game program he wrote over just four weekends. A Mason City, Iowa, college student wrote four game programs in one year and was rewarded with $150,000 for his brilliant efforts. A Tucson, Arizona, young married couple have reached millionaire status in less than four years writing game programs, and they "went into business" only as an extension of a hobby they so dearly love.

Not everyone can expect big money, but the profit potential is truly endless. Games offer the fastest rewards but are also the hardest to sell in a very competitive market.

The demand for new and well-written business and educational programs is increasing. Customers are demanding a wider level of program support along with well-written instruction manuals. The successful software companies must excel in all phases of production, marketing and support in order to survive. In the past, companies could get away with producing a sub-par product. Today's strong competition makes this impossible.

If you become a competent programmer, you can write and submit software programs to the various vendors. If you have no programming knowledge, you can teach yourself to program. Many good programmers were self-taught. I recommend that you stay abreast of the latest programming techniques by subscribing to programming journals and examining the software of others. These journals keep

75

abreast of new trends and what's currently hot. Joining a local "Microcomputer Club" in your area—and thousands of clubs have come into existence in the past few years—can provide you with a great source of new knowledge.

Before you spend many hours writing a new software program, you may wish to survey the market first. Find out what programs are in demand by talking to software vendors, computer clubs and individual personal computer owners. This will help you determine what to concentrate your time on for the greatest potential profits.

SELLING MICROCOMPUTERS

In 1982, over 1.6 million microcomputers were sold. Conservative estimates are that over 3 million were sold in 1983, and that well over 5 million were sold in 1984. Sales are soaring!

An obvious way to sell computers is to open your own computer store. This requires a substantial investment. A Radio Shack franchise (available from Tandy Corporation) will cost you in the neighborhood of $50,000 (dealership cost, initial inventory, etc.) plus building rent, fixtures and insurance.

A low-cost way to sell computers, ideal for the home-based entrepreneur, is to make sales without carrying inventory. There are several companies, both new and established, who will dropship hardware and/or software directly to your customer. No stock, no franchising fee and, hopefully, no hassles. These manufacturers can usually provide beautiful catalogs and professionally prepared brochures.

You can expect to earn 10% to 30% profit on your sales. Also, you may qualify for additional bonuses based on volume. Many of these companies also allow you to sign up other sales distributors and earn commissions on their sales via the multi-level marketing approach.

Here are three companies that market computers through independent distributors:

NOVATRONICS—full range of software—P.O. Box 7352, Minneapolis, MN 55407
TECHNICOM—computers and software—P.O. Box 15068, Salt Lake City, UT 84115
TRONICS—markets Texas Instruments computers and software—2536 E. Loop 820 Worth, Ft. Worth, TX 76118

Word processing and the microcomputer revolution offers the home entrepreneur almost unlimited opportunities to profit in new technology.

Probably the best book available on the subject of word processing is *WORD PROCESSORS AND INFORMATION PROCESSING* by Dan Poynter. This marvelous guidebook is designed to be used as a selection tool in purchasing word processing equipment, products and services. It also will give the reader a planning guide that will help determine your requirements plus an understanding of word processing technology. Add to this a comprehensive resource directory of available products and you have an important manual on this subject. You may order this great book by mail for only $11.95 plus $1.00 postage/handling from PARA PUBLISHING, P.O. Box 4232, Santa Barbara, CA 93103.

SOURCE DIRECTORY
COMPUTER MANUFACTURERS
(A PARTIAL LIST)

Alpha Micro
17881 Sky Park North
Irvine, CA 92714

Altos Computer Systems
2360 Bering Drive
San Jose, CA 95131

Apple Computer Inc.
20525 Mariani Avenue
Cupertino, CA 95014

Colonial Data Services
105 Sanford St.
Hamden, CT 06514

Applied Digital Data Systems
100 Marcus Blvd.
Hauppauge, NY 11788

Atari Computers
P.O. Box 61657
Sunnyvale, CA 94086

Basic Four Corp.
P.O. Box 11921
Santa Ana, CA 92711

Brother Industries
333 South Hope Street
Los Angeles, CA 90071

Burroughs Corporation
95 Horse Block Road
Yaphank, NY 11980

Canon USA
One Canon Plaza
Lake Success, NY 11042

Casio
15 Gardner Road
Fairfield, NJ 07006

Digilog Business Systems
Welch Valley Industrial Road
Montgomeryville, PA 18936

Hewlett-Packard Corp.
1010 NE Circle Blvd.
Corvallis, OR 97330

Information Systems
P.O. Box 1328
Boca Raton, FL 33432

Northern Telecom, Inc.
P.O. Box 1222
Minneapolis, MN 55440

Commodore Business Machines
487 Devon Park Road
Wayne, PA 19087

Compal Computer Systems
8500 Wilshire Blvd.
Beverly Hills, CA 90211

Compaq Computer
12330 Perry Rd.
Houston, TX 77070

Compucolor Corp.
P.O. Box 569
Norcross, GA 30071

Compucorp
1901 South Bundy Drive
Los Angeles, CA 90025

CompuPro, Godbout Electronics
P.O. Box 2355
Oakland, CA 94614

Data General Corp.
4400 Computer Drive
Westboro, MA 01581

Osborne Computer Corp.
26500 Corporate Avenue
Howard, CA 94545

Otrona Corp.
2500 Central Ave.
Boulder, CO 80301

Panasonic
One Panasonic Way
Secaucus, NJ 07094

Quasar Electronics
9401 West Grand Avenue
Franklin Park, IL 60131

Novation Corp.
18664 Oxnard Street
Tarzana, CA 91356

Ohio Scientific
1330 South Chillicothe Rd.
Aurora, OH 44202

Olivetti
155 White Plains Rd.
Tarrytown, NY 10591

Olympia
Rt. 22, Box 22
Sommerville, NJ 08876

Sony Corporation
9 East 57th St.
New York, NY 10019

Televideo Systems
1170 Morse Ave.
Sunnyvale, CA 94086

Timex Computer Division
P.O. Box 2655
Waterbury, CT 06725

Toshiba Systems
2441 Michelle Dr.
Tustin, CA 92680

Vector Graphic
500 North Ventu Park Rd.
Thousand Oaks, CA 91320

Quay Corp.
P.O. Box 783
Eatontown, NJ 07724

Radio Shack/Tandy Corporation
One Tandy Center
Fort Worth, TX 76102

Sharp Electronics
10 Keystone Pl.
Paramus, NJ 07652

Sinclair Research Corp.
Two Sinclair Plaza
Nashua, NH 03061

Tektronix
P.O. Box 500
Beaverton, OR 97077

Wang Laboratories
One Industrial Avenue
Lowell, MA 01851

Xerox Corporation
1341 West Mockingbird Lane
Dallas, TX 75247

Zenith Data Systems
1000 Milwaukee Avenue
Glenview, IL 60025

SOFTWARE HOUSES

(Write for their latest catalog.)

Aspen Software
P.O. Box 339
Tijeras, NM 87059

Broderbund Software
2 Vista Wood Way
San Rafael, CA 94901

Ashton-Tate
3600 Wilshire Blvd.
Los Angeles, CA 90010

Century Micro Products
P.O. Box 2520
Mission Viejo, CA 91690

Computer Exchange
P.O. Box 23068
Portland, OR 97223

Programming International
505 Hamilton Avenue #107
Palo Alto, CA 94301

Cornerstone Software
P.O. Box 5151
San Jose, CA 95150

Standard Software
CO-RI Bldg.
Avon, MA 02322

Designer Software
3400 Montrose Blvd.
Houston, TX 77006

Structured Systems Group
5204 Claremont Avenue
Oakland, CA 94618

800 Software
3120 Telegraph Avenue
Berkeley, CA 94705

Systems Plus
1120 San Antonio Road
Palo Alto, CA 94303

Lexisoft, Inc.
P.O. Box 267
Davis, CA 95616

Taranto & Associates
121 Paul Drive
San Rafael, CA 94903

Liberty Inc.
740 Main St.
Waltham, MA 02154

Vandata Business Software
17544 Midvale Avenue No. #205
Seattle, WA 98133

MicroDisk, Inc.
P.O. Box 1377
Gardnerville, NV 89410

Wholesale Suppliers
P.O. Box 22428
Carmel, CA 93922

Peachtree Software
3 Corporate Square #700
Atlanta, GA 30329

SOFTWARE BUYERS

Aardvark
2352 S. Commerce
Walled Lake, WI 58088

Manhattan Software
BX 1063
Woodland Hills, CA 91365

CDC
13715 Vanowen St.
Van Nuys, CA 91405

Powersoft
11500 Stemmons Exprswy., #125
Dallas, TX 75229

Instant Software
Peterborough, NH 03458

BOOKS

Basic Books
10 East 53rd Street
New York, NY 10022

Boardroom Books
500 Fifth Avenue
New York, NY 10110

Byte Books
70-P Main Street
Peterborough, NY 03458

Carnegie Press
100 Kings Road
Madison, NJ 07940

Gale Research Co.
Book Tower
Detroit, MI 48226

La Cumbre Publishing
P.O. Box 30959
Santa Barbara, CA 93105

Data Dynamics Technology
P.O. Box 1217
Cerritos, CA 90701

Datapro Research Corp.
1805 Underwood Blvd.
Delran, NJ 08075

Computer Book Club
Tab Books
Blue Ridge Summit, PA 17214

Computer Books
50 Essex St.
Rochelle Park, NJ 07662

Computer Reference Guides
2706 South Hill Street
Los Angeles, CA 90007

Essex Publ. Co.
285 Bloomfield
Caldwell, NJ 07006

Lifeboat Associates
1651 Third Avenue
New York, NY 10018

Micro Books
P.O. Box 6502
Chelmsford, MA 01824

Missouri Indexing, Inc.
P.O. Box 301
St. Ann, MO 63074

North Star Press
P.O. Box 1324
No. St. Paul, MN 55109

Datasearch
730 Waukegan Road
Deerfield, IL 60015

Prentice-Hall, Inc.
General Publishing Division
Englewood Cliffs, NJ 07632

Dekotek, Inc.
2248 Broadway
New York, NY 10024

Howard W. Sams & Co. Inc.
P.O. Box 7092-P
Indianapolis, IN 46206

Design Enterprises
P.O. Box 27677
San Francisco, CA 94127

Sybex
2344 6th St.
Berkeley, CA 94710

Knowledge Industry
701 Westchester Avenue
White Plains, NY 10604

Synergetics
P.O. Box 1077
Thatcher, AZ 85552

John Wiley & Sons, Inc.
605 Third Avenue
New York, NY 10158

COMPUTER PUBLICATIONS

Here is a list of leading computer magazines and journals, their approximate circulation, and the type of advertising they carry (display only, or display and classified advertising). Also, consider them potentially good sources of publicity, if you have something new and innovative to offer.

At, One Park Avenue, New York, NY 10016. 170,000 monthly. Display only.

Ahoy! 45 W. 34th St., New York, NY 10001. 125,000 monthly. Display only.

Analog Computing, 565 Main St., Cherry Valley, MA 01611. 100,000 monthly. Display only.

Byte, 70 Main St., Peterborough, NH 03458. 395,000 monthly. Display only.

Commodore Microcomputers, 1200 Wilson Dr., West Chester, PA 19380. Bi-monthly. Display only.

Commodore Power/Play, 1200 Wilson Dr., West Chester, PA 19380. Bi-monthly. Display only.

Compute! 825 7th Ave., 7th Floor, New York, NY 10019. 372,000 monthly. Display only.

Compute's Apple, 825 7th Ave., 6th Floor, New York, NY 10019. 150,000 monthly. Display only.

Computer Digest, 200 Park Ave., South, New York, NY 10003. 220,000 monthly. Display only.

Computer Shopper, 407 S. Washington Ave., Titusville, FL 32780. 100,000 monthly. Display and classifieds.

Computerland Magazine, 30985 Santana St., Hayward, CA 94544. 300,000 bi-monthly. Display only.

Creative Computing, 39 E. Hanover Ave., Morris Plains, NJ 07950. 255,000 monthly. Display only.

80 Micro, 80 Pine St., Peterborough, NH 03458. 91,000 monthly. Display only.

Information Industry Marketplace, R.R. Bowker Co., 205 42nd St., New York, NY 10017. Annual. Display only.

Mac User, 25 W. 39th St., #1102, New York, NY 10018. 100,000 monthly. Display only.

Macworld, 555 DeHaro St., San Francisco, CA 94170. 100,000 monthly. Display only.

Nibble Mac, 45 Winthrop St., Concord, MA 01742. 22,5000 - 6 times a year. Display only.

Online Today, 5000 Arlington Centre Blvd., Columbus, OH 43220. 185,000 monthly. Display only.

PC, One Park Ave., New York, NY 10016. 230,000 bi-weekly. Display and classifieds.

PC Tech Journal, One Park Ave., New York, NY 10016. 82,000 monthly. Display and classifieds.

PC World, PC World Communications, Inc., 565 Dettaro St., San Francisco, CA 94107. 538,000 monthly. Display and classifieds.

Peanut, 545 Fifth Ave., New York, NY 10017. 100,000 bi-monthly. Display only.

Personal Computing, 10 Mulholland Dr., Hasbrouck Heights, NJ 07604. 540,000 monthly. Display only.

Popular Computing, 70 Main St., Peterborough, NH 03458. 262,000 monthly. Display only.

The Processor, P.O. Box 578, Webster City, IA 50595. 32,000 weekly. Display and classifieds.

The Rainbow, Falsoft Inc., 9529 U.S. Hwy. 42, Prospect, KY 40059. 76,000 monthly. Display only.

Run, 80 Pine St., Peterborough, NH 03458. 180,000 monthly. Display only.

Sextant, 716 E St., S.E., Washington, DC 20003. Bi-monthly. Display and classifieds.

Small Business Computer News, 140 Barclay Center, Cherry Hill, NJ 08034. Monthly. No advertising.

MORE PROFITS WITH YOUR PC

Lawrence Carter of Brooklyn, New York, is a master teacher on how to earn huge profits with a PC. He has recently written an inexpensive short course on this subject. Mr. Carter has been selling my books for some time, and I'm happy to recommend his new PC Profit Course. Without obligation, write to him for free details: Lawrence Carter, Carter Publications, Inc., 65 Eckford St., Brooklyn, NY 11222.

MLM—NETWORK MARKETING—A HOME-BASED BUSINESS WITH GREAT POTENTIAL

The fabulous success of companies such as Amway, Mary Kay Cosmetics, Herbalife, and other multi-level marketing leaders, has proven the MLM—Network Marketing concept can produce big profits, and in a hurry for both the prime company and the person who jumps on the right bandwagon.

Therein lies the dilemma. To make a bundle in MLM, you must choose the "right" company. Almost any type of product or service can be marketed on a MLM marketing basis. To profit, we must select a solid company with a good product or service. In recent years, a lot of "grab the money and run" opportunists have become active in MLM.

SELECTING THE GUYS WHO WEAR THE "WHITE HATS"

In the world of network/Multi-Level Marketing, there are good guys, bad guys, and others somewhere in between right and wrong. Even more important than the product or service you are hustling are the people with whom you are aligned. To make money both quickly and securely, you want to cast your lot with a company that has knowledgeable, solid, innovative, and honest management. *A great management team is essential to your success.*

Learn all you can about a company, and its top people. At the top will be a handful of men and/or women who will control the entire destiny of the company. You want to be with the good guys, the ones with the pure-white Stetsons.

One reason the term Network Marketing has replaced Multi-Level Marketing in some circles is because a lot of questionable characters without staying power, ethics, class, or good products have tarnished the term MLM.

You may get rich in MLM Network Marketing, but it will only happen if you're honest and associated with an honest and reliable marketing company.

SELECT A GOOD PRODUCT

Several multi-marketing setups do offer good potential profits; however, it is important that you do not get involved in a chain-marketing or chain-letter scheme that is illegal. While we cannot offer any legal opinion here, a key point seems to be that a bona fide product or service must be involved. Sending money back and forth to people, when no real products or services are received for payment rendered, is usually characteristic of an illegal "chain" operation.

Big success in multi-level marketing is more often the result of establishing dealerships than the actual product or service involves. By setting up a long line of dealers, you share in their success and receive commissions on their sales. However, the product should also have real merit and be in demand. If the product or service cannot be sold on its own merits, chances are that the company—and everyone associated with it—will fail.

86

THE MULTI-LEVEL CONCEPT

Regardless of the product or service offered, the concept behind multi-level selling is hooked into the recruiting of as many new distributors as possible to continue to sell the product or service.

Let's say you get in early on a five-level, multi-level marketing deal. As an example, let's say you're promoting Aloe Vera juice (very much in demand today!) and your basic selling unit is four quarts (one gallon) for $20. And let's suppose you are allowed to keep $5 out of every $20 sale you make. This is level one. Now, let's say that you will be allowed $1 on every order your distributors make on levels two through five.

Here is an example of the amount of money you could make if you signed up only four distributors who, in turn, duplicated your efforts. Using the hypothetical figures outlined above ($5 profit per original sale and $1 commission on the next four levels):

Level #1—You acquire 4 and receive $5 each............$20
Level #2—Your 4 acquire 4 each......................$16
Level #3—These 16 acquire 4 each $64
Level #4—These 64 acquire 4 each $256
Level #5—These 256 acquire 4 each $1,024
TOTAL: $1,380

Within a very short time, with only four people duplicating your sales production, you could earn $1,380 from a very minimal effort of only four sales (multiply this by only 10 times and the number becomes $13,800).

Sounds great, doesn't it? And sometimes it even works that well—but not always. It is unlikely that a minimum effort of only four sales with distributor setups would hold up so well through five levels. Multi-level marketing experts tell me that you have to set up ten distributorships, on the average, to get one outstanding "go-getter" who will prove to be an outstanding source of "downline" commissions.

Sign up two hundred or more active distributorships and you may actually get rich. The fast money-making potential here is brain-boggling!

Multi-level selling originally centered around household products sold in person, house-to-house, or through party-plan selling, but now it has entered the world of mail order, too. Some network/MLMs sell exclusively by mail. Others only sell face-to-face, while still others use a combination of both methods.

THE SKY'S THE LIMIT

The sky really is the limit when you talk about the profit potential of Network Marketing. One million dollars, or more, in just one year, is possible. Several MLM companies are now claiming that 20% of all new millionaires in America, during the past several years, obtained their great wealth through Network/ML Marketing. This dynamic marketing concept may soon overtake real estate investing as the prime means of reaching millionaire status.

BEWARE OF ILLEGAL PRODUCTS

The exchange of money, with the absence of any product or service, is usually a chain scheme that is illegal. Another major consideration for you, if you intend to get into multi-level selling, is the legality of your product. It is wise to shy away from companies that are making outlandish claims regarding their goods. If it all sounds too good to be true, it probably is. Be extremely wary of products which make exaggerated "health cure claims." The Food and Drug Administration and the postal service tend to take a dim view of such operations. Although you would probably come under the heading of "Independent Contractor," and not be considered an employee of the company's headquarters, you still could be subject to harrassment or even prosecution if you are distributing (in person or through the mails) products or information that are deemed to be harmful or dangerous or grossly misleading in nature.

If the proposition in question troubles you, stay away from it. If it seems just too good to pass up, consult an attorney for a legal opinion.

GET THE FACTS AND FIGURES FROM "THE HORSE'S MOUTH"

If you are anxious to learn more about the kinds of services and products, plus profits, that are available through the Network Marketing approach, the following partial list of leading distributors and/or prime sources of multi-level marketing organizations can furnish you, without obligation, full information on the merits of their programs. Write to several or all of them; look over the wide range of products, services and specials available; compare the various marketing plans (mail order, networking, party selling, etc.) and "projected earning schedules" before making your decision. Give special consideration to the plans, the products, and the management team. The right choices could help you make a fortune.

When writing any of these firms, simply ask that they send you details on their multi-level marketing program.

Following is a list of firms who offer a wide variety of products and services sold via various multi-marketing plans. They are listed here as sources of information only. While I personally feel that they all offer marketing plans that are sound, legal and beneficial, I cannot guarantee it.

A.L. Williams Corp.
3120 Breckenridge Blvd.
Duluth, GA 30199
(insurance marketing)

Ideal Products Inc.
P.O. Box 1238
Everett, WA 98206
(large line of cosmetics
& consumer products)

American Liberty Productions
1640 Miland
East Alton, IL 62024
(long distance phone service)

Innovative Marketing
P.O. Box 22822
San Diego, CA 92122
(many different programs)

AMWAY Corporation
7575 E. Fulton Rd.
Ada, MI 49355
(Amway products)

The Kronia Group
8223 Southwest Cirrus Dr. #17
Beaverton, OR 97005
(Spicers International Products)

Charles G. Possick
Box 59001
N. Redington Beach, FL 33708
(many different programs)

Mary Kay Cosmetics
8787 Stemmons Freeway
Dallas, TX 75247
(cosmetics)

Earth Fragrances
P.O. Box 26291
Raleigh, NC 27611
(fragrances)

Shaklee Corp.
444 Market St.
San Francisco, CA 94111
(large line of consumer products)

Herbalife International
5741 Buckingham Hts. Pkwy.
Culver City, CA 90230
(Herbalife diet & health
   products)

Uncle Charlie's Products
2215 29th St., S.E., Suite C
Grand Rapids, MI 49508
(coffee & other consumer
   products)

MLM BOOKS

Here are some good books about MLM/Network Marketing that can further your knowledge about the opportunities that are available.

ALL ABOUT MULTI-LEVEL MARKETING, The Wave of the Future, by Jan Cunningham. This is a wonderful new book for people who are new to MLM/Network Marketing and want the facts and figures, and the straight scoop. You'll get a great MLM education for only $12.95 postpaid. Order from: CMC Multi-Level Marketing, 1020 15th St., Suite 41C, Denver, CO 80202.

Would you like to be the next MLM millionaire? Charles

G. Possick, who has been associated with Multi-Level Marketing for many years, believes he can help you make a ton of money. He has a two-volume set of manuals, entitled *MLM Secret Manuals*, available. Possick knows MLM inside out, and this set of manuals could be very valuable to you. Available for $20 postpaid from: Charles G. Possick, Box 59001, N. Redington Beach, FL 33708.

THE MAGAZINE OF THE INDUSTRY

Anyone serious about making big money in Multi-Level/Network Marketing will want to subscribe to *Multi-Level Marketing News*, 10236 Fair Oaks Blvd., Fair Oaks, CA 95628. Write to them for current subscription information.

HOME TYPING

This is probably the most common home business of them all—typing at home! Your only equipment and supplies are a good quality machine and a supply of paper and related accessories. Profits are not spectacular but they can be steady.

Home typing can include a huge assortment of typing-for-pay activities. Here we list a few of the more profitable plans:

(1) General Typing: This includes letters, forms and circulars for small businessmen, attorneys, etc. The market is any and all owners of small businesses, or professionals who either (a) do not have enough work for a full-time secretary or (b) have too much for their current secretary. To solicit business, small ads can be run in local newspapers, notices placed on bulletin boards in various retail stores and laundries, and/or circulars and flyers circulated to ALL (remember that almost any retail business or wholesale business of professional office is a potential customer)

possible clients. Printing shops can be a great source of business.

(2) Resume Typing: This can be an ideal typing home business all by itself or combined with other typing activities. The job market has become more competitive during the early 1980s and those people seeking the better jobs must submit attractive resumes. If you're not familiar with resume layout and typing (clients will furnish details about their past education and employment history, but you will have to put things in order, lay out each resume and type it in logical order), there are several excellent books available at your local library. Business can be obtained from small ads in newspapers. Also, place ads in college papers and on campus bulletin boards. Prior to graduation, students can be an excellent source of business. Also, send details of your services to any professional organizations in your area. Professional people make more job changes than the average worker and have great need of professional resume services.

(3) Typing information for State, Federal and County Courts: All courts employ reporters who use shorthand (at speeds of 200+ words per minute) to record their proceedings. Once a shorthand record is made, these court recorders either type up this information themselves or dictate their notes into tapes and have someone else transcribe them.

Rates vary from city to city, state to state, but are usually in the 50¢ to $1.00 per page range.

How fast you type does not matter here (at least not to the courts since they are paying per page—not per hour) except to earn decent money ($1,000+ per month) you will need speed. What is critically important is accuracy and good vocabulary. Misspelled words or poor grammar are not tolerated here.

To obtain business, go to your local courthouses (city, county, state, and/or federal) and see as many court reporters as possible. Your state's "Legal Directory," available at most libraries, can also be a rich source of contacts.

Although doing legal typing for lawyers is not exactly the same as doing business with the courts, it can be a related source of extra profits. Attorney offices are a vast source of typing business.

(4) Home typing for publishers and mail order companies. Many publishers and mail order firms use home workers on a regular or semi-regular basis. Get in touch with these companies in your area.

The above forms of home typing represent only a tiny fraction of the huge volume of typing available. Just remember: Any type of business or profession is a potential customer. Another great thing about running a home typing business is you can get started very cheaply (less than one hundred dollars will rent a good typewriter and supplies), and you're able to work as few or as many hours per week as you choose. Of course, your profits will depend on how many hours you devote to your home business as well as how fast you can accurately type. Forty or fifty words per minute may be okay for starters, but to make your home business really profitable, you should raise your speed to eighty words per minute, or more.

Profit Range: Can range from $0 or $50 to $300 or more per week, depending on your ability to solicit business and put in the time to turn out the work. Again I say, not a get rich business, but a popular business that is very easy to start.

HOTLINE: TELEPHONE PROFITS

Direct marketing (mail order, direct mail, direct response radio and television, etc.) is booming in America today. Americans always have loved to shop at home and the trend is increasing.

93

Although most folks continue to send in their orders or inquiries by mail, an increasing number of people are shopping by phone. We have all seen the TV commercials that tell you to call this 800 number to order your records, books, gadgets, or whatever! When you're in the order- and inquiry-taking business, it is your phone number flashing on the screen or being given by the announcer or appearing on printed matter.

This booming industry offers anyone a great home-operated business (although many of the larger firms do rent office space). Burgeoning entrepreneurs are making substantial profits. Start-up costs can be initially limited to the installation of two WATS lines from Ma Bell to handle calls from the state you live in and one to take calls from the rest of the nation.

PAY PHONE PROFITS

The breakup of Ma Bell has fostered a telecommunications revolution. Now we have MCI, Sprint, Express Tel, and a hundred other competitors. More important to the small, home-based entrepreneur, is the new wave of moneymaking opportunities available in pay phones.

You can ring-up big profits from pay telephones at convenience stores, restaurants, gas stations, donut shops, and other small businesses that generate heavy traffic. There is big money to be made in this field.

USA Today recently said, "There are millions to be made owning pay phones." The *New York Times* calls pay telephones "one of the most promising investment opportunities for the decade." *Fortune* says "customers drop $350 to $400 a month into a typical gas station pay phone." Vending machine expert Shel Klein states, "A pay telephone is the best new profit idea in vending machines in the last 20 years!"

In recent years many states have legalized private ownership of pay telephones. An FCC ruling has legalized these
phones; the FCC's Common Carrier Bureau Chief says the
ruling means a private pay telephone may be placed
anywhere interstate calls may be made from the phone. Calls
within a state are to be regulated by each state's public
utilities commission.

Each state differs, so you must know local laws. If the
conditions are right, this could be a tremendous moneymaker.

Here are three companies who offer pay telephones and
marketing plans. You may wish to write for more information.

Your Nickle   Tonk-A-Phone
P.O. Box 609   P.O. Box 388, Shoreline Blvd.
Laveta, CO 81055   Spring Park, MN 55384

Capital Tel Systems, Inc.
305 Fairfield Ave.
Fairfield, NJ 17006

CLAIM YOUR SHARE OF THE
TWENTY-FIVE BILLION-DOLLAR
OPPORTUNITY

While most of the home business opportunities in this
book offer moderate to outstanding profit potential, very
few, if any, can match the profit-potential of this one.

Make up to two thousand dollars an hour just for looking
up people's addresses? Is this really possible?

"Yes, it's possible to make that kind of money," says
author David Bendah. Well, I think David is a good guy, but
still this is an incredible claim. I decided to do some research.
My research led me to a small company in Phoenix who took

in over a million dollars last year, doing essentially what David talks about in his new book. Over one million smackers, and most of it clear profit!

Here's the story: It has been estimated that there is twenty-five billion dollars waiting to be rediscovered in America. Money citizens have forgotten or lost in bank accounts, stocks, insurance premiums, etc. This is money that ends up in the state treasury, so it stands to reason they do not knock themselves out to find the right person or the individual heirs.

David Bendah has developed a money-making system that will allow you to make lots of money quickly by finding people and sharing the money they have coming. David says, "If you would like to make up to $2,000 per hour for just looking in some phone books, this could be your great opportunity."

After looking into this money-making concept in detail, I'm convinced it is a legitimate get-rich opportunity—one of the most incredible and revolutionary money-making opportunities ever presented.

I recommend that you read Dave's eye-opening new book, and act quickly. I have a sneaky feeling that the states may someday soon change the laws, and prevent entrepreneurs from making sensational profits while helping heirs claim money that is rightfully theirs. After all, most politicians are eager to get their hands on more money, not let it slip out of their grasp.

To order your postpaid copy of this remarkable book, *$2,000 an Hour*, send a $10 check or money order to:

Dave Bendah
6602-B El Cajon Blvd.
San Diego, CA 92115

IMPORTANT DATES

A housewife in Akron, Ohio, earns "an extra $40 to $45 per week" using this little number, on a spare time basis.

Half the population has poor memories when it comes to important dates in their lives (birthdays, anniversaries, engagements, etc.)

The plan is simple: A small classified ad in daily papers lets people know that for a small fee a postcard will remind them in advance (usually one week in advance) of important dates. A supply of postcards plus a handy file index plus a few dollars puts one in business.

Opinion: You won't get rich fast with this one but the small profits come pretty easy and you can "get into business" for $25 or less. A good tie-in with a telephone service.

FANCY WRITING
FOR FANCY PROFITS

Mary Ellen Johnson of Milwaukee, Wisconsin, made over $50,000 last year doing ornate lettering for publishers, restaurant owners (menus), sales awards, educational diplomas, etc.—fifty grand a year with only a couple hundred dollars worth of supplies working out of her own home. Initially, she invested a little money in advertising. Now she has more business than she can handle via word-of-mouth. Over 90¢ on every dollar she earns is net before tax profit!

Originally a dental receptionist, Mary Ellen learned her craft during two years of both night school and private lesson calligraphy classes. Her advice to others interested in making money through ornate writing, "If you already write and print clearly, you can learn calligraphy." Old English is probably the most in-demand form of scribe writing. No, it is not simple, but it can be mastered.

At $50,000 per year, it is a skill worth looking into.

QUESTIONS AND ANSWERS BUREAU

We all seem to have questions that we would like answers to. Many of these questions require research that not everyone has time for, or at least, thinks he or she doesn't have time for. A Phoenix, Arizona student has turned people's questions into super part-time profits. Ed placed an ad in both the daily paper and his college weekly, advertising that he would research questions at a rate of $2 per question and up. Response was greater than anticipated. Within a few weeks, profits of $200 to $250 were obtained on a spare-time basis!

Startup capital is practically nil ($20 to $50 to place a few small ads). Most research is done at the local public library, although Ed says he tries to check out reference material whenever possible so as to keep his business in his apartment. His claim of $10 (average) per hour of research makes this an attractive home enterprise.

CASH FOR CARTOONS

Even if you think you have no art calling or drawing ability, you still could learn this highly-specialized calling.

You don't have to have great artistic talent to learn cartooning. What is more important is a sense of humor and an outrageous outlook on life. Sure, the ability to draw a tree that looks like a tree (not a lollipop!) and your males and females should be distinguishable, but really, imagination and creativity are your greatest assets.

Leaf through current magazines and newspapers. Clip out all the cartoons you find (and you will find many). Decide

(A) which type (political, social, slapstick, etc.) you like best or (B) which type you think you can do best.

The tools of the cartoon trade: Supplies include ordinary pencils, sketch pads (a good grade 20 to 25 pound with 20% rag content is desirable), some brushes, ink and a drawing table (these can be rather expensive, especially a "lighted table," but you could build your own). Lots of famous cartoonists, and many more not so famous, started out with only a breadboard or a simple chunk of plywood.

Desire: As is the case with the writer, you are not going to be a cartoonist unless you have a burning desire to do so.

Money to be Made: The real pros earn up to a thousand a week (many without leaving their home), but the vast majority of cartoonists do something else to earn their main income and delight in occasional sales to various print markets.

You should be able to find several good books on the subject at your local library.

SELL A CARTOON COURSE

Once you master the art of cartooning, or even if you never do, you can make money selling a cartooning course. Here's how Debbie of Dallas, Texas did it.

Debbie's friend Joel was a very talented artist who also was a first-class cartoonist (the two do not always go together). Joel in turn had a buddy, Rob, who could write well. The two fellows had talent but little promotional ability, and that's where Debbie made her mark. Debbie knew many people were interested in cartooning, so she formed a three-way partnership with Rob and Joel to put together a course.

Her plan involved putting together a 180-page course (oversized, 8½x11 format). Ads are placed in local newspapers and college newspapers. A 500 press run cost our trio $1,950. Within 90 days they sold all 500 manuals (called "courses" for effect) at $24.95. That's $12,475 less $1,950 printing and $1,800 advertising, which left $10,725 to be split three ways.

Obviously, anyone with all three talents, (1) promotion, (2) cartooning and (3) writing and a couple thousand for printing could do it all and reap all the profits, provided that they were as creative as Debbie.

ENTERTAINMENT BUREAU

If you live in or near a good-sized city (one hundred thousand plus), you may be able to earn great fulltime or part-time money by establishing an Entertainment Bureau.

To work this plan, you must contact as many musicians, dancers, comedians, ventriloquists, hypnotists, etc as you can find. You then audition them to be certain you're dealing with people with some talents. Once you have gathered several "acts" who agree to give you 10% or 15% (go for 15% if you can get it!), you can represent them.

To line up bookings you must have printed letterheads and envelopes, circulars or brochures advertising the group and rate cards. Send these to nightclubs, social clubs, churches and charitable organizations soliciting engagements.

A little-known technique that can work wonders: Put special emphasis on social and fraternal clubs, churches and other non-profit organizations. Work to line up dates with these rich sources of tailor-made (through their membership) audiences in which they will receive a split (usually 50-50) on all revenue that comes in. These groups will often be very pleased to produce a large turnout when they realize a good hunk of the proceeds will come to them.

We know of two partners in St. Louis, Missouri who

started out from scratch in 1979 and in just two years grossed $250,000 with their talent agency. The profits are out there for anyone who has a flair for promotion and who is willing to work with and for various artists who, at times, are somewhat temperamental.

Successful Entertainment Bureau promoters soon may find themselves working closely with big stars. We know of one San Diego agency who started small and who now is engaged in booking dates for country stars such as Willie Nelson and Anne Murray. You must walk before you trot and trot before you run. However, in this entertaining business, you can rise to the top fast if you possess real promotional ability and enjoy working with creative people.

This kind of operation could be listed under "spare time business" as well as "home business." It is usually wise to get started on a part-time basis.

INVENTORS REP

In every city and hamlet in our nation, many local inventors are eager to market their brainchildren. If you have real promotional skills, you can earn lucrative profits by representing and assisting them in their marketing desires.

You can, without spending a lot of money, establish an inventors' bureau; publicize the inventions and act as an "inventors agent" in marketing. Inserting a small advertisement in your local paper announcing your services will secure you a list of inventors. They generally seek such assistance. You can also be of invaluable marketing assistance by studying the invention, determining who would most likely desire to buy it and then contacting these sources, either by mail or in person.

Similar services normally charge up to five hundred dollars and more for invention "evaluation" plus 10% to 15% of all proceeds that result from your marketing contacts. You will have no problem obtaining many creative clients if you launch this home business by offering substantially lower rates. We have recently heard of a Los Angeles, California man who got started from scratch and earned $30,000 net profits in his first year with his own Inventors Bureau.

VOCATIONAL COUNSELING

People nowadays are constantly switching jobs and vocations. This has created a potentially lucrative, fulltime or sparetime business that can be operated out of a home office.

Mary Jane Kramer of Seattle, Washington started a vocational counseling service in Seattle a few years ago on a part-time basis and has seen it develop into a $25,000 plus per year business.

She first performed this service among her friends and subsequently advertised in publications of mass appeal. She offered to give complete vocational analysis for a low fee. Upon receiving the application, she would submit a questionaire, requesting data on the applicant's age, schooling, present job, etc. This data enabled her to gauge the qualifications of the writer and to offer suitable vocational advice. Consultation of various psychology books yielded much information concerning questionaires, vocational adaptability and other necessary subjects that aid her in her booming profession. She charges twenty dollars for each analysis and now has a waiting list of new clients and has even had to hire a retired school teacher to work parttime to assist her.

Our analysis indicates this business is tailor-made to the changing job market of the 1980s.

Following is a group of home businesses that concern themselves with arts and crafts, gardening, food and cooking...

BRAID RUGS

Americans have been indicating new interest in handmade rugs. Rug-braiding is not difficult and can be learned as easily as knitting. The materials are quite reasonable and there is an expanding market for them. Once you learn to produce braided rugs in a reasonable amount of time, you could expand into doormats, knit purses, potholders, chairpads, etc., all of which are less time-consuming than rugs.

There are several fine firms that will be happy to supply you with materials and instructions.

Write:

Barclay
170-30 Jamaica Avenue
Jamaica, New York 11432

Adams and Swett
380 Dorchester Avenue
Boston, Massachusetts 02127

Heirloom
38 Harlem Street
Rumford, Rhode Island 01916

Your markets include department stores, hobby and craft shops, boutiques, rug shops and related outlets. You can also mail-order your wares through ads in craft magazines. "Needlepoint" is the leading magazine in this field.

Potential profits are good as you often can mark-up your rugs and other accessories four to five times your raw cost for materials. Even by allowing a 50% discount to retail stores, your profits can be substantial.

DESIGN HATS

Custom millinery—hat-making—is an ancient art practiced from the time of the Egyptians to the present date. For the man or woman who enjoys sewing, likes working with her/his hands and who keeps up with fashion, this creative art can earn attractive profits.

To get started, save all fabrics, feathers, beads, material, blocks, ribbons, bows and nets—you can use them all. Books on hat-making can be found in libraries and bookstores, and once you have read up on techniques you can, if you wish, begin. If you want to study millinery, inquire at the local millinery shop about courses given or learn from a friend. Study the hats at boutiques and see if you can duplicate them. Study at home can also be arranged. For information write:

Academy of Millinery Design
1500 Cardinal Drive
Little Falls, New Jersey 07424

The Academy supplies you with the tools and the materials necessary to begin.

Where to sell your hats? At the millinery shops, ladies' clothing shops, special orders for weddings or for women's clubs, crafts shops, theatrical-costume shops. You can also consider giving courses yourself once you are a master of the hat universe and teach others this little-known art. As this is being written, the current hat craze in America continues to be western headgear. Sharp designers are getting up to $100 and more for their one-of-a-kind western hats.

FURNITURE UPHOLSTERING

Homemakers, offices, hotels and motels all use the services of upholsterers. This can be the ideal work out of your home business, parttime or fulltime.

How to begin? First, be certain that upholstery is your scene. It requires certain tastes and certain talents. You must like fabric and the tactile sensations; you must have a feeling for furniture; you must have a color sense; you must enjoy seeing your hands at work. If all these check out, go to it. Upholstery is not limited to simple recovering—you may be called to hang drapes and sew them, make slipcovers or pillows, do automobile upholstery and basic furniture repair and the like. If you decide to learn upholstery at home, contact:

Modern Upholstery Institute
Orange, California

If you plan to work at home, a good idea is to upholster your own living room and use it as a showcase for your work. The Modern Upholstery Institute will also help you—they provide advertising for you and a kit that includes business invitation letters, a mailing-list guide, business stationery and forms and a business advisory service. One nice thing about this trade is that it allows a husband and wife to work together at home as a team.

Amount You Must Spend? The course from the Upholstery Institute costs $238 ($215 if the full sum for tuition is paid at once). The course includes many of the basic tools, but the rest must be purchased separately.

Amount You Can Make? Working parttime can still bring in as much as $150 a week. To reupholster one couch takes two or three days, and you can charge from $75 to $100 for the work.

ART AND CRAFT BROKERAGE

A bright young California couple, Steve and Shannon of Newport Beach, live in a beautiful seacoast village that has become a colony of artists and creative craft workers. While most of these people are high on talent, they generally are not so blessed with business knowledge. Enter Steve and Shannon!

Steve and Shannon had been party-plan sales people for years but were looking for a new, profitable and stimulating enterprise. They found they could relate well to the artists and craft people in this seaside village, and they outlined a marketing plan that suited many of the creative people.

Shannon and Steve load up their VW van once per week with the crafts, sculptures and art and head down the freeway to selective shops, stores and boutiques in the Los Angeles area. Special emphasis is given to the posh shops in wealthy Beverly Hills.

Steve and Shannon operate a "cash on delivery" business with their established network of retailers.

They keep 25% of all sales as their commission. "We were lucky to make $50 or $60 a week when we got started last year," Steve informed us, "but now we often earn $400 to $500 per week. Not bad for less than ten hours of work per week." We call it great!

Not bad at all. Anyone living near an arts and crafts center or near almost any big city could organize a similar distribution setup.

GROW ORGANIC VEGETABLES

The natural food movement that got into full swing in the 60s and 70s is definitely going to continue and increase during the 1980s. Today people are more aware than ever of the dangers certain sprays, colorings, dyes, refining and preservatives present. The health-food market is experiencing record growth.If you have some land (even ⅓ acre can produce a vast harvest using modern growing techniques) and a green thumb, you can turn your green thumb into long green cash.

How to Begin? If you have done any gardening, there is really little that must be learned or changed in order to grow organic vegetables. Seeds taken from organic vegetables are considered to be organic seeds. Start from there. When your vegetables start to grow, you treat them with natural sprays and fertilizers that protect the produce completely and at the same time leave them untainted by any poison or artificial chemical. Today you will have little trouble selling your organic foods once they mature. People drive miles to obtain them, and the only thing you need to do is spread the word. If you've sold vegetables in the past, so much the better. You can sell from roadside stands, at your house, to the local markets or on consignment. For information on basic organic gardening, write for the book list from:

> Rodale Press
> 33 East Minor Street
> Emmaus, Pennsylvania 18049

To obtain the names of the various suppliers of organic materials, look at a copy of Rodale's magazine Organic Gardening, which costs $1 on the newsstand. Two other good suppliers of organic materials are:

> National Development Co.
> Bainbridge, Pennsylvania

> Vita Green Farms
> P.O. Box 878
> Vista, California 92083

While profits will vary depending on the yield of your ground and your ability to produce a bountiful harvest, we have heard of folks earning up to $7,000 per acre of land.

FLOWER POWER PROFITS

A green thumb plus a salesman's license is all you need to enter this home business. And don't despair if you live in a house or apartment with no room for a flower garden. If you can sell this blooming product, local suppliers will be available to you.

There are many ways to peddle beautiful flowers (roses and

carnations are two of the most popular varieties, but several others qualify also for fast sales). Any good, busy street corner (with or without flower cart) can yield a gross of $100 or more per day selling your flowers in $2 and $5 bunches.

Here's another technique that is red hot. We have heard of a flower peddler in Houston, Texas who earns up to $1,000 net per week with this little jewel. This entrepreneur hires attractive young women to sell his roses (he buys them at wholesale since he is not a grower) in popular restaurants, bars and clubs in the Houston area. We are told he splits the profits with his pretty salesgirls, but with a group of six to eight attractive "flower girls," his profits soar. You may want to look into this. Even if you're not a grower, a $5 "bunch" of flowers will probably cost you $1.50 or less, leaving you an excellent mark-up, even if you hire others to help you make sales. Caution: Flowers do perish quickly. Do not buy or grow more than you realistically believe you can sell. If you're buying wholesale from a grower, it's often wise to buy a fresh batch daily rather than to purchase several days supply. Nobody buys cut flowers that have wilted.

KITCHEN CANDY
PROFITS

Bess Peterson of Duluth, Minnesota makes the best fudge east of the Mississippi River. Ask any of her relatives or friends who receive "fudge baskets" as birthday or Christmas gifts. Only a few years ago did she take her "heavenly fudge" public. A niece who opened her own restaurant finally talked Bess into placing some of her fudge in neatly wrapped packages at the counter of her breakfast and lunch diner. Her fudge was an instant sensation. Soon other establishments were clamoring for her fudge. Bess went into business, but only to the extent that she could remain in her kitchen (thank goodness, Uncle Bob enlarged it by another

300 square feet)!

Now, in addition to fudge, Bess also makes her delicious brownies available to the good folks in the Duluth-Superior area. She could double or triple her business if she wanted to. A candy and cookie distributor wanted her to increase her business and give him an exclusive on the Minneapolis-St. Paul market. But Bess refused. She is already "earning more money than Uncle Bob and I need, and we don't want to work longer hours. If folks in the twin cities want my brownies and fudge, they'll have to drive 100 miles to Duluth."

Well, so much for Aunt Bess. She has as large a share of the "kitchen market" as she wants. God bless her.

Many old family recipes can launch a super home business. Some of the greatest tasty food items never make it to the marketplace. As important as good food items are, the ability to promote them is just as vital. Since the great cook is not always the great entrepreneur, often times a partnership is called for.

If you have an Aunt Bess in your family who has a great food dish, or a mother or grandma who has a "secret recipe," why not get busy forming a kitchen partnership that can make mucho money for you both. Good food items can become an overnight success when strong marketing strategies are employed.

It is often smart to begin your technique by "test marketing" your food item at a handful of selected stores or restaurants. Then, based on these results, you can plan a more ambitious advertising and marketing campaign.

An Important Tip: Try to keep control of your product during the early going. If it proves to have national appeal and you don't have the capital to launch a national marketing campaign, you can arrange to sell out at a profit. First prove its appeal; then decide if you want to maintain control or whether you (and your famous cook) will take your profit and let someone else carry the ball.

MAKE ORIENTAL RUGS AT HOME—
PROFIT THREE WAYS

Thanks to a progressive manufacturing company in Hong Kong, you can create your own oriental rugs; the kind that sell for $100.00 to $500.00 at auctions, exhibit shows, flea markets, etc.

You can profit from this machine in three profitable ways:

(1) Manufacture oriental rugs and sell them yourself.

(2) Manufacture oriental rugs and sell them to wholesalers, stores, flea market dealers, swap meet sellers, etc.

(3) Sell the machines and materials to people who would like to make money at home.

For information on the machine and materials write to:

Kin Yuen Metal Engineering Works
36 Sung Chi Street, G½F
Hung Hom Kowloon, Hong Hong

RENT FENCES

Pilferage is a big problem on "on the job" sites. Workers steal 10% to 20% of the goods that disappear. A bigger problem is the 80% to 90% carted away by outsiders. Construction sites are among the hardest hit.

In 1967 Anthony Ortega, who owned a small fencing company, came up with a bright idea. He approached a local housing project and offered to put up a cyclone fence for a nominal fee. "If my fence doesn't cut down pilferage, I'll leave it there free for a year." The construction boss took Mr. Ortega up on his offer. Soon after the fence went up, he admitted on-site thievery was drastically reduced. Thus,

Ortega's "Rent-A-Fence" business was formed. Offices are now all over the nation.

For more information write to:

Rent-A-Fence
1236 East Los Angeles Ave.
Simi Valley, CA 93063

GOLDEN PROFITS FROM
THE GOLDEN GATE

When the Golden Gate Bridge authority decided to replace the heavy duty suspension cables on the Golden Gate Bridge after they were in use over forty years, a group of San Francisco entrepreneurs went into action. They bought the old cable, sliced it into 4-inch chunks and successfully sold them as momentos of San Francisco's past at $35.00 to $50.00 per chunk.

$35.00 got you a plain piece sitting in a leather covered presentation tray. For $40.00 you could get a chrome plated piece and for fifty dollars you received a gold plated chunk. Each chunk was numbered and represented a true collectors item. Close to two million chunks were sold. You figure up the amount; it is really overwhelming!

Now what does this have to do with you? Think about it! The day will probably come along in your area when a historical site will be demolished or taken down. Old parts of historical value, be they bricks, stones, wood, rail or chunks of cable from a bridge, are very saleable to collectors.

Original material brings the biggest bucks, but don't overlook "authentic replicas," either. The state of Illinois made a tidy profit recently when they first took down and sold their old Route 66 signs and later when they produced and sold thousands of Route 66 sign replicas.

111

WEALTH-BUILD WITH LOG HOMES

History has a way of repeating itself. Who would have ever thought that log homes would be back in demand in 1987? After all, this "primitive" form of building was big in 1784! Believe me, today the log house has returned.

As housing costs continue to soar (the average price of a new home today is fast approaching $100,000) many Americans and Canadians are returning to relatively inexpensive dwellings that once housed their ancestors.

You will find log cabins in the rural areas and you will also find them in suburban Cleveland, Chicago, Minneapolis-St. Paul, Dallas-Ft. Worth, or just about anywhere a home owner wants a sturdy, low-price shelter. In the great state of Kentucky, log homes represent 2% of all new construction.

While some log homes are built from chopping down nearby trees, many more are purchased in pre-assembled kits. In addition to considering a log home for your dwelling, profits can be made in both selling them and contracting for their construction.

Four of the leading suppliers of log home kits are: Lincoln Homes, Box K, Rt. 152, Smithfield, OH 43948; Natural Log Homes, Rt. 1, Box 164, Noel, MO 64854; Smokey Mt. Log Homes, P.O. Box 549, Maggie Valley, NC 28751; New England Log Homes, P.O. Box 5056, Hamden, CT 06518.

MAKE BIG BUX IN
THE BLOOMING HEALTH FIELD

The College of Life Science says, "You can quickly master this 100% effective health system of Life Science, and help overcome ailments such as acne, asthma, tumors, diabetes, heart ailments, high blood pressure, overweight, backache, venereal disease, psoriasis and almost anything else."

The college offers a nutritional science course and doctorate degree and will show you how to be a Ph.D. in just one year.

The college publishes a dynamic monthly magazine. "Healthful Living" plus a newsletter, "The Health Science Newsletter." They offer many health-related programs. If interested, write for full details to: College of Life Science, Manchoca, Texas 78652.

Another institution offering ways to profit as you serve is the Holistic Massage training course available from: Kripalu Center for Holistic Health, P.O. Box 131, Summit Station, PA 17979.

200 hours of residential training in one of the nation's leading holistic care centers will equip you for a certificate in meditative massage, reflexology, acupressure point work and other related therapies. And that certificate can launch an exciting new vocation. And one that can be performed in your own home.

Many women, and several men too, are earning up to $50 an hour as massage therapists, often from a spare room in their home. Qualified massage schools have opened in major cities nationwide. This is an occupation with a profitable future.

BELIEVE IT OR NOT:
THEY PAY FOR DUST!

Hollister-Stier Laboratories, 3525 Regal St., Spokane, WA 99220, has a problem—the company gladly pays cash money for common, everyday house dust to the tune of 50¢ a pound. That's a fact! The problem is, convincing folks that they will buy dust! Most people cannot believe anyone would pay money for something most homeowners would like to rid themselves of. The company presently buys dust from five collection points in Yeardon, PA; Downers Grove, IL;

Atlanta, GA; Dallas, TX; and Burbank, CA. Paper bags or vacuum cleaner sacks are the preferred means of collection. Plastic trash bags are not desirable because the dust in them tends to get too moldy.

If you can convince yourself that this firm means business, you can reap some easy profits.

The amount of dust in an ordinary vacuum cleaner bag is worth $1.50 or more.

Remember, they buy dust and not dirt (that would be too easy). The average household will net a tidy sum. However, you will have to collect dust from other sources to really cash in big. Perhaps you could run a little ad offering to pay, let's say, 25¢ a pound collecting dust from others or how about making a deal with a large janitorial service? The possibilities, like dust, are endless.

VINYL REPAIR PROFITS

Here is a nifty part-time or full-time occupation that can be run from your home or your garage—repair vinyl. At home earnings can range from $20 to $30 an hour.

Wallace Brown of Mankato, Minnesota reports one job that required repair and recoloring of six booths. "It took two of us three days and was close to a $4,000 job." Those kind of earnings demand attention.

Vinyl PRO, 436 West Hopocan Ave., Barberton, Ohio, 44203, has a process approved by Ford, General Motors, and Chrysler. The company claims that you can get started with them for less than you can make on your very first job.

To find out how you can cash in providing this in-demand service, write the company and request full details on how you can make good bux in vinyl repair, recoloring and refinishing. The company says information is FREE and no sales person will ever call.

Another company offering a genuine money-making opportunity in the vinyl repair field is Vinyl Industrial Products, 2021 Montrose Ave., Dept. 7, Chicago, IL 60618.

We know of a husband and wife team in El Cajon, California, who are doing extremely well in this business. It may be worth your while to look into this.

LET THE IRS
HELP YOU MAKE MONEY

Today the Internal Revenue Service takes a big chunk out of every dollar you make. Too big a chunk methinks, but that's another subject. My point here is that you can actually make a handsome income preparing tax forms for others. Some training is required, but once you have the knowledge you can earn steady income at home and with a little cost-effective advertising, folks will beat a path to your door.

Imagine going into business with a powerful money-hungry partner (IRS) who develops customers for your service year after year. It is estimated that 90 million people filed 1982 taxes and that at least 30 million of them paid an outside service for professional assistance.

Knowing how to prepare tax forms is important, but equally vital is promoting services to people in your community. A Chicago company (Federated Tax Service, 2021 West Montrose Ave., Chicago, IL., 60618) specializes in teaching ambitious homeworkers how to do both. Write them for free information on their fast-learning tax training and practical methods for obtaining business. You don't have to be an accountant or mathematical whiz to make money preparing tax forms.

115

BE A CONSUMER HERO
AND MAKE MONEY, TOO

Here's a powerful money making concept from Robert J. Sturner, founder and director of "People's Discount Club Of America." Economic conditions are ripe for this plan. Mr. Sturner claims a man or woman can earn $500 per day part-time while saving consumers huge amounts of money on their everyday spending. At the same time merchants greatly increase their business.

We have looked over this plan and feel it does have real potential. P.D.C.A. now has "clubs" in all 50 states plus several foreign countries. They have been in business since 1976 and are the largest discount club in the world. Obviously, Mr. Sturner and company are doing many things right.

For more information on this organization and their money-making plan, write:

Robert J. Sturner
People's Discount Club of America
7216 Manzanita Street
Calsbad, CA 92008

VIDEO TAPE WEDDINGS AND
OTHER SPECIAL OCCASIONS

Luna Video of Los Angeles, California, has found success in video taping weddings and other special events; so can you.

Brides and grooms enjoy a permanent record of their special ceremony and reception and are willing to pay handsomely to have their day of bliss recorded for posterity.

I believe this service will continue to boom in the years ahead. Video taping also lends itself to other services.

Recently several people have pre-recorded their last will and testimony. Other events: graduations, confirmations, baby christening, etc., also offer good profit potential. Within a few years almost everyone will have a disc player hooked up to the TV set.

While I believe that with the necessary equipment and a flair for promotion, anyone could set up their own business, it also may be wise to get help from a pioneer in the field who can help you avoid the pitfalls and give you a shortcut to success.

For free information, write: LUNA VIDEO, PO BOX 85324, LOS ANGELES, CALIFORNIA 90072.

BLOW UP YOUR PROFITS

Making fast cash is child's play when you sell popular helium balloons. Working out of your home, you can earn up to $50 or more an hour selling at shopping malls, fairs, bazaars, parks, flea markets, swap meets, beaches, parks, churches, schools, carnivals, stadiums, arenas, even standing on a busy street corner or in the lot of an active corner gas station.

Majorie Miller of Sacramento, California, earned a good living with a small flower stand. When she added a line of popular balloons to decorate her stand, as well as to earn additional profits, she was amazed that she soon was selling more balloons than roses!

Listed below are three leading firms you can contact if you are interested in balloon selling:

CREATIVE BALLOONS, INC., PO BOX 1165, CARMEL VALLEY, CA 93924

SILVER SALES CO., 671-13 MILE ROAD, SPARTA, MI 49345

ACME PREMIUM SUPPLY CORP., 4100 FORREST PARK BLVD., ST. LOUIS, MO 63108.

COUPON CLIPPING

Now let's give you the lowdown on a dynamic new 1980's concept to make fast cash, easy!

Manufacturers of "cents off" coupons began turning up everywhere during the late 1970s (in newspapers, magazines, as well as inside or on the backside of boxes of merchandise). America has gone "coupon crazy," and this trend is expected to continue for several years to come.

Here's how a Chicago woman has turned this boom into a windfall of profits! She finds her local paper carries $10 to $15 or more of "cents off" coupons in the food section, once per week. She buys several papers and clips every available coupon. She then sells these coupons to grocery stores, usually the independents, at about 15 cents on the dollar. Fifty newspapers with $15 worth of coupons in each one of them would yield $750 at face value, which in turn would net her $112.50 (15% of $750). Her only cost would be 25¢ times 50, which is $12.50, the cost of the papers. Even this can be reduced if friends and relatives will save papers for you.

While not all merchants will buy, this Chicago lady has found there are enough who will to make it more than worthwhile to clip and clip. She believes they use these "cents off" coupons to offer to their customers. $100 profit from about two hours "work" adds up to sweet profits.

Opinion: It is illegal for you to send in coupons for cash refund, unless you are selling the products named on the coupons. Using this plan, you simply sell to stores and the responsibility becomes theirs. We believe this is legal but suggest you consult your attorney to make certain you're not violating any laws, should you decide to use this plan.

118

SEMINARS IN THE HOME—
MONEY IN THE BANK!

The thirst for knowledge on thousands of different subjects by millions of people has created a booming new home enterprise—seminars/workshops in the home for adults!

What type of home seminar could you offer that people, in small groups, would pay for? Chances are good that you, like most folks, have valuable knowledge on one or more different subjects that people would gladly pay to receive.

Here is just a brief sampling of the home based instructions now being given here in my "backyard" (the San Diego area):

Home based classes, seminars, workshops, etc., currently include: Language skills (Spanish is the most popular, attended by people from the Midwest and East who have recently moved to Southern California), Rapid Reading and Recall, Solar Heating Information, Interior Decorating, Car Care For Women, Protection from Violence, How to Properly Use Firearms, Public Speaking, Negotiation Skills, Hairstyling, Advanced Makeup Techniques, Skin and Eye Care, Modeling, Male-Female Relationships, How to Cope After Divorce, Initiating Relationships, Touching, Overcome Shyness, Creative Writing, Portrait Drawing Instructions, Watercolor Painting, Hand-formed beads, Sewing Skills, Batik, Pine Needle Basketry, Photography, Acting, How to Operate Your Own Business, Bookkeeping for Beginners, Typing Skills, How to Incorporate a Business, How to Start a Business, Consulting, Country Western Dance Lessons, Gourmet Food and Wine Course, Meditation, Sailing, What You Should Know About Casino Gambling Before you Go To Las Vegas...and that's just for starters!

Are you beginning to get the picture? The only people who probably do not have special information that many others want to obtain, are people who have lived their life in a cave somewhere!

The fees charged for home-based instruction vary greatly. I know men and women who hold occasional classes in their homes or apartments for a "little extra spending money" monthly ($100 to $300 per month), while others have turned their home seminars into a full-fledged enterprise, raking in thousands monthly by holding several classes or seminars each week. Fees range from $5 to $50 per attendee for each session (usually 2 to 4 hours in length.)

Advertising for attendees need not be expensive. Small ads, even classified ads in daily and community newspapers work well, and some dollar-conscious entrepreneurs obtain free advertising by tacking up circulars in laundromats, grocery stores, and other places where people congregate. If you do a good job teaching people skills they want to learn, much repeat business will be forthcoming via word of mouth. Size of groups who attend home classes/seminars vary, but most instructors feel less than six is too few and more than 15 is too many, per session.

A NEW CONCEPT IN TRAVEL AGENCIES AND VACATION EXCHANGING

The high cost of travel and the slow economy of the past few years (1981-1983) has brought "hard times" to many traditional travel agencies. However, this also can mean opportunity for home-based entrepreneurs.

Alternative travel can become popular since high costs have driven potential globe trotters into looking for a better and cheaper method in which to get from here-to-there. The idea here is in the sharing of private vehicles and resources.

There is a real need for an agency to mastermind and coordinate this kind of travel. When you consider the millions of cars, planes, trucks, boats, motor homes, etc., owned by private citizens, you begin to comprehend the fabulous profit potential available.

The key here is to play travel matchmaker. Matching people looking for travel, facilities, lodging, etc., with those who can provide the services, equipment, and facilities required, for a fee.

Acting as a clearing house, the operator of the alternative travel agency charges a fee for matching clients.

For example, let's say a driver is going from Los Angeles to New York—He lists his or her origin, destination and date of departure with your agency, agreeing to pay a fee if you can place one or more people who are interested in traveling with him/her to share expenses. Fellow travelers need not travel every mile of the trip—although this may be desirable—the driver also could pick up riders who paid you a fee to list their travel needs in cities along the route. In this example from Los Angeles to New York, many cities in several states would provide pick-up and drop-off spots along the way.

Then you have a second listing (and fee) from this driver on his return trip from New York to Los Angeles a few weeks later, repeating the process lining up riders.

The fees you charge can be determined on distance, or you may opt for a flat rate. Naturally the people providing the transportation will have to base their charges on distance traveled. Using our New York to Los Angeles example, let's say both the driver and rider paid you $25 each for your service, then the rider paid the driver $75 in transportation fees, he or she would be able to make the nearly 3,000 mile trek from Los Angeles to New York for only $100, less than ½ the price of traveling by bus and only about ⅓ the air fare cost.

CHECK REFERENCES—If you decide to book alternative travel, you must absolutely check references. Your clients have every right to anticipate a safe journey with a "normal" rider or driver. Although you will take reasonable precautions, you must get a disclaimer form printed so that it relieves you of any responsibility for accidents, thefts or other problems between the parties.

PRIVATE AIRPLANES

Anyone who pilots their own aircraft could offer the same service as auto drivers. Many business persons fly regularly, owning or leasing their own planes; many would welcome other business persons to share expenses. On the other side of the coin, many business and sales people, professionals and general travelers would be happy to share expenses with a pilot who can give them time saving and money saving air transportation. Here again you could provide a valuable service to both.

MOVING TOGETHER

More people than ever are renting their own trucks and moving themselves. As an "Alternate Travel Agency" you could match people who wanted to share a large truck or van to a common destination, or a location along the route. Since it is cheaper to return a van (round trip) than to pay for a one way trip, you could arrange for booking the return. If two parties moved from Seattle to St. Louis, you could arrange for one or more parties in the St. Louis area to return the van to Seattle—all parties paying you a nice fee for your match-up services.

TRANSPORTATION AND LODGING EXCHANGES

Exchanging of vehicles and residences is another profit source for anyone starting an alternative travel agency. People in Minnesota who wanted to visit the mountains of Colorado would exchange their lake front home and auto for a Rocky Mountain condo and car.

Vacation home exchanging is already gaining popularity throughout the free world. Arranging such exchanges between Americans could net big profits, with the possibility of going international in the future. This type of service could match people all over the world. America is the nation most foreigners want to visit and Americans love to travel almost anywhere.

Getting into this business will not cost a fortune. Advertising and promotion is the key to success. Ads in the travel section of large metropolitan newspapers, plus direct mail could build volume quickly. Word of mouth from satisfied clients can help keep business rolling. Although this type of business could start almost anywhere, I do believe a major city would offer a better chance of gaining quick recognition. A smaller town, but one near a desirable vacation area—lakes, the mountains, tourist attractions— should also work well.

Your fees must be reasonable enough to attract clients and at the same time substantial enough to afford you a decent profit. While there are many ways to handle fees, it may be wise to handle your services in a fashion similar to the activities of an ad agency. Fees are determined by individual listings. It is reasonable not to charge the same fee for someone exchanging vacation homes in, let's say, New England and New Mexico, as you would for someone who only wants a ride from Milwaukee to Chicago—less than a one hundred mile trip.

A low membership fee to help process paper work, listings, check of references, etc., may also be a great idea.

A basic fee for each particular type of service could be established, based on the value of the service. Advance payment of all fees is a must. Get paid before any travel or other services are performed. A small computer to keep track of various services offered and desired, plus application processing would be required once volume picked up. A card filing system probably would suffice for a few months of operation.

There is real potential here. The concept may need more fine tuning, but I really believe several entrepreneurs can develop a big money-maker from the alternative travel, rental and vacation sharing business.

This type of business can be operated from your home on a part-time basis. Later you may wish to expand into a downtown office space.

The possibility to set up a network of agencies in major cities is real and this concept would also lend itself to franchising and national/international promotions.

This kind of opportunity is definitely not for everyone. Let your imagination run wild and give it some serious thought. It may be just right for you!

BUYING AND SELLING
ALMOST ANYTHING!
BUY CHEAP—SELL HIGH!

No one ever lost money buying cheap and selling high. It is another basic philosophy of mine that I have personally prospered with! Don't allow the simplicity of this statement to throw you, it is a proven wealth-building approach.

Wheeler-dealers are making big money today. Bargains are available in good used items and closeout new merchandise.

(1) Attend all available closeout sales (not the kind held by retail stores, but the kind offered by wholesalers and distributors—look for "closeout notices" in the classified section of large metropolitan newspapers). Also shop all nearby auctions, garage sales, flea markets and swap meets, searching for good under-priced used merchandise.

(2) Use the "shotgun" approach to under-priced buying. Buy almost anything that is grossly under-priced, if you believe you know where to peddle it at a substantial profit. Space

may be a consideration. Don't load up on items that will require expensive storage.

(3) Also, use the "rifle" approach. While being willing to buy almost anything at a super low price, it is usually wise to find a niche in the market. Start specializing in specific goods to a defined market. Your specialty could be used cars, typewriters, office equipment, tires, furniture, jewelry, antiques, rare coins, stamps, books, art, clocks, bikes, electronic gear, appliances, television sets, or whatever else turns you on and lends itself to a quick resale at at least double what you paid for it!

In spite of a somewhat depressed economy, bargains are still available if you dig for them. In fact, you're surrounded by them!

How much money can you make buying and selling? Easily a couple thousand dollars per year on a very limited basis. I have known some very active, very sharp "horsetraders" who make up to fifty thousand dollars a year in steady buy-sell transactions. The sky is really the steady limit. Your income will only be restricted by (A) the time you invest in your buying-selling activities, and (B) by how well you can spot super bargains and then turn them over at substantial profits.

IMPORTANT BUYING GUIDELINES

(A) PURCHASE ONLY MERCHANDISE FAR BELOW MARKET VALUE. A "good buy" is not "good" enough. You want a fantastic bargain! A friend of mine buys and sells used, reconditioned typewriters. It has become a very lucrative sideline business. He runs little ads in various newspapers and shoppers guides:

WANTED *used typewriters, must be in good condition.* CASH. *Phone –000-0000*

He receives dozens of calls from eager sellers each week, almost all of them offering to sell a good machine at a reasonable price. He recently told me, "I could make a substantial profit with about 90% of the machines people wish to sell me. However, I don't want a good deal, I want a GREAT DEAL! By only purchasing about 10% of the typewriters I am offered, I generally triple my money and am still able to give my customers (he sells to both individuals and businesses) a bargain price—way below!!!" There are enough "highly motivated" sellers around—people who want fast cash money—that you can buy goods at huge discounts.

(B) KNOW THE VALUE OF WHAT YOU BUY. Don't put yourself in the "trick bag" by buying items that you "think" are at bargain basement prices. It is vital that you know the approximate value of anything you purchase. You will often have to make a fast decision and may have to make an "educated guess," just make darn certain you can "ballpark" the potential value. I knew a fellow who once bought 5 gross (720) "mood rings" at *25¢* each. He had bought a similar mood stone ring for his wife a few years before at $5, and reasoned he was making a fantastic buy. What he didn't know was that the "mood ring" craze had burned out and his rings were in little demand. He was unable to find a jeweler or novelty store to buy the rings, even at his break-even price of .25¢ each. He finally sold them to various California swap meet sellers at his cost, but considering his time and effort to get rid of his rings, it was a losing proposition.

The lesson for all of us who buy and sell goods; Know today's approximate values and stay away from "fad" items that are at the tail-end of their selling cycle.

(C) KNOW THY MARKET! It's only a great buy if you know where to sell it at a great profit. While it is not absolutely necessary to know who your exact buyer will be, it is wise to have a darn good idea where to locate your potential buyers. This factor alone makes a strong argument for the selective approach to buying and selling. Don't buy ANYTHING that you don't have some idea as to where and how it can be sold!

126

PYRAMID YOUR PROFITS

While many moneymaking ventures require several thousands of dollars to get started, not so with my "grass roots" buying and selling strategy. You can get started for "peanuts" and pyramid your profits—fast. I have personally bought small items (watches, tools, etc.) for less than $50 total and sold them for $300 within one week. If you reinvest most or all of your profits during the first few months, you can turn a "chicken-feed investment" of only one hundred dollars or even less into many thousands in a very short time. And the beauty of this is, you can devote as little or as much to your buy-sell activities as you desire while running your regular full-time business or working at your regular job.

Buying and selling is the basic, profitable, independent, home-based business. It's free enterprise with a capital F! It is easy to start, requires very limited funds and offers you truly unlimited potential!

My advice: Get involved! It's fun and profitable.

PROFITS FROM PLANTS

Janet Murphy's home is a veritable jungle of palm and fig trees, hanging ferns, ivy plants, spider plants and other assorted lush green plants, succulents and begonias. Janet has a sweet green thumb and she is cashing in on her talents with her own interior plantscaping business. The only thing that seems to be growing faster than her many plants is her bank account.

Miss Murphy's customers include both small and large offices, restaurants, and an indoor shopping mall.

People like to be surrounded by plants and other foliage because they personalize business establishments, soften appearances of otherwise sterile doctors' and dentists' offices and "dress-up" any location with their color and charm.

127

Working out of her lovely southern California home, "two thousand square feet, but the plants have taken over fifteen hundred," she informs you she has parlayed her magic thumb and an original capital investment of only two thousand dollars into a green business with a deep black bottom line. Could this be a home-based opportunity for you?

Although Janet does not service residential clients, I have heard of others in this blooming business who do—specializing in providing plantscaping for upper middle class and downright wealthy people. It has been reported to me that one couple who specialized in plantscaping for the nice, rich and refined folks of Beverly Hills, California, earn over a hundred grand per year working out of their home. That seems quite high, but there is no debating that plantscaping offers relatively low risks and high profit potential.

PLANTS TO STOCK

The key to success in this business is to handle the type of plants that hold up well and require only minimal care. All of the multi-varieties of the dracaena family (including dracaena marginate, a beautiful tree-like plant) do extremely well and are readily available. Fig trees (ficus) are always popular for their leafy, weeping effect. Palms are also always in big demand. Many clients choose the smaller, less expensive plants or trees. Boston fern and asparagus fern are very popular for hanging baskets, even though they are a bit finicky and require additional care.

PLANT DESIGN

Although designs can be standardized, every home, office or commerical area presents unique advantages and/or problems. The plantscape designer must consider lighting, temperature, humidity, traffic density and space limitations.

PLANT SOURCES

Most people who operate a plantscaping design business buy their stock from local growers. You will discover that most nurseries carry a large variety of plants and trees. Once you really get your fledgling enterprise off the ground, you can consider buying plants and trees from leading wholesale nurseries in Florida. There are shipping companies who specialize in bringing plants from Florida to all parts of the USA. Once you establish credit, orders can be placed with Florida growers by phone.

Caution: Any nursery who ships plants is only responsible for plants until they are loaded on a truck. You must check with people who have already used the trucking services to be sure you are dealing with a reliable transporter.

People who enter this potentially lucrative enterprise soon discover that it is wise to use sterilized artificial soil for potting. Too often the soil in your backyard is contaminated with undesireable organisms (nematodes, grub worms, ants, fungus, centipedes, and bacteria), which can eat or decay your plants. Organic material such as vermiculite also should be added to your potting soil to make it looser and more aerated.

PLANT MAINTENANCE

Although substantial original profits are obtained from initial plant sales, your business will probably require plant maintenance services in order to thrive. These are the "bread and butter" of the business and include such services as pruning, fertilizing, watering and spraying.

It is usually wise to offer various "service contracts" to clients. One contract can be for basic maintenance: water, spray and fertilize if necessary. Plants are maintained under this agreement but usually without any guarantee. A monthly fee of $20 to $50 for weekly service is reasonable, and is dictated by how many plants a client has.

A more elaborate contract which guarantees the plants—offering replacements as needed, would out of necessity demand much higher monthly charges. It is not uncommon for a large establishment with many plants and trees to pay up to $300 monthly for guaranteed care.

The prices you charge for interior plantscaping to earn a profit depend on the "on-site" considerations. If nearby windows offer plenty of sunlight, plant care will be quite easy. Many establishments do not afford this ideal atmosphere. You must figure the wholesale value of your plants and the probable loss over a year (which can be as high as 20% in some places) and your time, effort and supplies involved in your plant care. Don't overlook or underestimate unusual circumstances. Some plantscapers are required to climb ladders to hang and water plants in high ceiling restaurants, office buildings, and homes.

Your hourly wage should be penciled into all service costs. Only you can decide how much per hour your time is worth, but the range seems to be from $12 to $30.

Chances are that it would not be worth your time to charge less than $20 or $25 monthly to any client, including a single family home.

The best way to estimate any job is to figure all wholesale costs, including your overall cost of operating your business and then adding what you consider to be a fair profit. It is recommended that you add 50% to your overall costs to put your business in black ink and keep it there.

Plantscaping can be started as a one-person operation. Later you may wish to expand and hire others to help you. Since basic service and maintenance skills are learned quite easily, the going rate for hired help is quite low, in the $5 to $8 per hour range. If you don't provide transportation (a van is an excellent vehicle in this business and can be leased at a substantial tax write off) you will have to pay any assistants you hire an extra transportation allowance for providing their own transportation.

It can also be a smart idea to bond yourself and any employees you hire. It assures customers that you are trustworthy. Liability insurance is a must both on the site and in transit to jobs.

An excellent source of important information for prospective plantscapers is the Interior Plantscaping Association, 1601 Washington Plaza, Suite 14, Reston, Virginia 22090.

Many universities are offering courses in horticultural design. Also, your local library is a rich source of horticultural information.

GOURMET PROFITS
FROM CATERING

Staying in the kitchen at a party while everyone else is drinking, eating and having fun, may not be your idea of a good time, but it certainly can be profitable.

The new breed of social caterers often earn a net income of $200 to over $5,000 for their orchestrated planning and culinary expertise. Americans love to eat and be entertained and those folks with enough money to indulge will pay handsomely to have their special dinners and parties planned, prepared and served within their own homes.

Many people who love to dine out and be entertained have been turned off by fine restaurants which are overcrowded and impersonal. Several have found it is better to "bring the restaurant" into their homes.

Here's a home-based business that can bring home the big lettuce for people who like to work with food and who have a flair for promotion.

AN EXPANDING FIELD

Today social caterers offer everything from breakfast in bed for two, to lavish dinner parties for 200. Although still a relatively new concept, great expansion is underway and anyone wanting a big slice of the pie should get established as soon as possible. And yes, you can get started in your own home.

LUNCHEON OPPORTUNITIES

In the past, business people limited their lunchtime catering to placing a call to a local deli and asking that "a certain number of salami sandwiches and hot or cold drinks be sent over." While this practice still continues, more and more business executives are going first class. Enter the personal caterer.

The secret to success in catering is to get paid BEFORE the food and drink is purchased and prepared. The host or hostess must inform you in advance how many guests are expected and pay either half (50%) or all of your total charges several days before the luncheon, dinner or party. Thus, you can use the client's money to cover all or most of your services.

HOW TO GET STARTED

The first thing a professional caterer must do is know how to plan. Advanced planning, right down to the smallest details is required for success. Printed forms that give you a check list on all planning, preparation and serving can be an invaluable helpmate. Last minute surprises only cause hassles.

Perhaps the best way to do the cooking is right in the client's home. However, some clients do not allow this, demanding that the food be prepared elsewhere. Naturally, you absolutely must prepare business conference luncheons in your own home or elsewhere. This is usually no problem, as cold salads, sandwiches and snacks often comprise luncheon servings.

Personalized service is a must! The caterers who are making the really big money have found out success comes as much from catering to the host or hostess as their guests. Clients love personalized service and being made to feel very important.

In addition to providing the food and service, some professionals arrange for the liquor, soft drinks and juices, and hire bartenders—sometimes even musicians and other entertainers, etc. One successful Seattle catering service specializing in astrology parties, complete with special zodiac decorations, etc., also brings a professional astrologer with them to entertain guests. Another service in San Jose has turned a handsome profit in specializing in the catering of bridal showers, with appropriate decorations and a hired photographer. A specialty can often help a beginning caterer get into business quickly with minimum advertising and promotion costs.

Should you decide to go into this business you will need promotional skills every bit as much as the ability to plan, prepare and serve delicious food.

Your local librarian can point you to several books on the subject of catering. This can be a super profitable business to enter, but in the final analysis it is the kind of business that requires you to offer personal service in which your own personality and organizational ability will determine your success or failure. It is a business that can be operated from your home without regular employees. Most caterers cultivate a list of people who work as independent contractors to prepare food and serve it on a party-to-party basis.

DELIVERY SERVICE SUCCESS

Susie Skates, popular ex-model and San Francisco-style entrepreneur, keeps in super shape and is making lots of money in her home-based business.

Susie swoops along San Francisco's winding sidewalks delivering messages and small packages. She charges $10 and up per hour for her unusual delivery service. At 6-foot-1, wearing a pink mini-skirt and on skates, Susie gets attention—lots of attention.

Skating several hours a day isn't all fun. "It's hard physical work," Susie confesses. "But I enjoy talking to people. Everyone is just so nice," she grins.

They obviously enjoy it too. "I skate in, blow my whistle and say, 'Here's a message for so-and-so!' and people are always so surprised that they start laughing."

Susie admits she started her business by accident. "I've always enjoyed roller skating and would skate miles a day to and from a waitressing job I had.

"One day my boss offered me an extra $5 to make a delivery to a special customer who lived a mile away. I said 'sure' and roller skated all the way there in no time.

"When I got there, the man who was handicapped, offered me another $5 to deliver a package to a friend. It so happened that the house he wanted it brought to was right on my way home so that was really easy money.

"I started asking around the business district and found there were a lot of small places that had deliveries to be made but didn't want to pay the exhorbitant prices regular delivery places charge.

"Before I knew it I had dozens of clients calling wanting me to make deliveries at all different times. It got so the only

134

way I could handle the demand was to quit my job. I was getting more jobs every day. As soon as I quit, I began making more money.''

Now, before you invest in skates, short pants or mini-skirts (hey, this could be fun, but also dangerous!), let's develop this idea, making it more plausible for the normal Joe or Jane. (Not that Susie is abnormal. She and her specialized service are just very unique.)

Local package delivery services are sprouting up all over the nation. We know a guy in Pasadena, California who started with one van—his own personal transportation—and built his delivery service into a very big and profitable business. Currently he has five vans and one large truck and a profit of over $115,000 last year! Another young lady in Atlanta, Georgia started very small a few years ago and now has more business than she can handle. But to meet the big demand, she continues to expand.

With an insured van or station wagon, or even just a car, you can get started making money quick (if Susie does it on skates, even a little VW gives you an advantage).

First, find out the services and pricing of your local competition. Next, visit your insurance agent and get bonded. Since you can start home-based you should be able to charge 10%-35% less than most of the competition.

While ads in the phone book and local newspapers can help build business, personal contact is also vital. Have a printer run off a batch of flyers and drop them off at major retailers and offices throughout your area (this home-based business is suited for a mid-size to large-size city). Be certain to contact all attorneys in your area, as they often need legal documents delivered to their clients and/or the courthouse. Large real estate offices and escrow firms also use this type of service repeatedly.

Delivering packages and messages on roller skates may not be for you, but a home-based delivery service, using more conventional transportation, could put you in the pink!

MAKING MONEY WITH TOYS

If you like to make things with your hands, you may want to consider making toys. They are always in big demand and profits can be spectacular.

There is an ingenious California family who is making big money by turning a toy-making hobby into a lucrative money-producing business.

Starting out on a shoestring budget, the Sindledecker family is getting rich by making things in a one-room manufacturing plant that also serves as their home.

On a typical day, Kathy and Glen Sindledecker and Glenn's brother Steve can be found working away on imaginative toys in the back room of their home. And after school, Kathy and Glenn's 8-year-old son, Tom, helps out in his specially designed task of pounding wheels onto toy trains, cars, and trucks.

The dynamic group is regularly coming up with complete lines of toys for all ages. Their products include cars, trucks, planes, boats, trains, and construction equipment like road graders and cranes. They make adult toys, a complete gas station, even the Starship Enterprise, all made out of wood.

They make all sizes of hobby horses, a best seller among their adult customers. Other adult products include an executive flip-flop car that will do a somersault on a desk top as well as conversation pieces such as elaborately constructed nutcrackers and pencil retractors constructed with wooden gears and pullies and chains.

The Sindledeckers attribute their success to their parents, George and Helen Jackson of Whittier, California, and Wayne and Sally Sindledecker of West Jefferson, Ohio.

136

With their parents offering help over the years, Kathy and Glenn are now doing what they want to do.

In fact, the business is proving so successful that Glenn has been able to quit his high paying job at IBM to devote all his time to the toys.

Kathy, Glenn, and Steve all attend classes part-time at Antelope Valley College in Lancaster. After class they start the table saws, drills, and sanders working in their toy shop. And then, on weekends, they attend arts and crafts shows in various parts of the state to market their wares.

Although their workshop is about the size of a one car garage, it includes such items as a floor model drill press (which they use for all drilling operations) and two belt sanders. One is a disk sander, the other an old band saw converted into a sanding belt. There's also a radial arm saw and a band saw.

In between all the equipment are work benches and shelves piled high with toys waiting for new owners. There are also stools and a pile of sawdust that is hauled outside on a regular basis.

For materials, the family goes to various lumber mills where they either buy or are sometimes given end cuts and regular odd stock lumber.

Kathy will cut out the toy and hand it to Glenn to drill. Then Glenn will sand the sides, followed by Kathy getting the toy back to complete the inside. Then Glenn will cut into the wheels and give them to Kathy to sand. Together they assemble the final product.

"Teamwork is what makes our business work," Glenn said. "It's easier for us than for someone else, because we enjoy what we're doing. That's one of the most important considerations if you're going to start your own business. You'll have a hard time making it if money is your only consideration."

The Sindledeckers are not alone in manufacturing toys at home. Clyde and Candy Allmond of Colorado Springs, Colorado make teddybears and other stuffed animals in their home. The energetic couple (they work 50-60 hours per week to meet the demand of individual customers and stores that stock their creation) quit their jobs (he a former postal clerk; and she, a former secretary) and retired to what Clyde says is, "lots of hard work, lots of fun and twice as much money as we used to make."

Raymond and Marcia Sanchez of Sacramento, California are making substantial money by making plastic "superheroes and science-fiction characters" at home, selling them both locally and by mail. Four teenagers, two boys and two girls, are their only employees.

What do the Sindledeckers, the Allmonds and the Sanchezes have in common? Creative ideas and a love for producing their own creations.

Toys are big business, a multi-billion-dollar business in America alone. If this home business interests you, visit your local library, looking through the Thomas Registry found there. Here you will find sources for any supplies you need to make toys in your home. Of course, if all the ingredients you need can be locally obtained, so much the better.

How much money can you make in the toy or game manufacturing business? The potential is truly unlimited. Let me tell you the unusual story of Mr. Erno Rubik. It's a real-life, very recent rags-to-riches story that should get your creative juices flowing. Mr. Erno Rubik is the man who gave the world the famous *Rubik's Cube*.

In 1974 Erno Rubik, an obscure, absentminded professor of architecture and design in Hungary, began fiddling with a curious little wooden model that he had just constructed. He had conceived this tiny multicolored cube, with its 26 rotating "cubies" as a teaching aid to help his students understand three-dimensional objects.

138

Try as he might, he could not restore the puzzle to its pristine state in which each face is a single color. And try as he might, he could not stop trying. He became infatuated with his little creation, obtained a patent on it, and in 1977 licensed a state trading company to sell it. It soon became a national mania throughout Hungary, addicting over 2 million people—one-fifth of the population bought the cube.

Rubik offered it to several large American toy manufactures in 1978. Incredibly, they all rejected this cube. Finally, Ideal Toy agreed to carry it on trial, and in just two years the cube has driven over 10 million American cubists to distraction.

Since he has a patent on his cube, Rubik is paid a royalty for every one sold anywhere in the world, and its phenomenal success has catapulted him into the unique position as perhaps the only self-made millionaire in the Soviet Union.

BOARDING PETS

If you have the space to keep dogs and cats and other animals, this can be a lucrative business. Be sure to check local zoning ordinances.

With so many people now traveling so much of the time, pet boarding has become big business in recent years. And the fee charged for boarding is steadily rising. Here in San Diego, pet boarders are charging $5 to $10 a day ($25 to $30 a week) to board a cat or small dog, and much more for larger breeds.

You'll need pens and kennels, and that will cost some money to get started. You also must keep your boarding area neat and clean. Owners want Fido in a friendly, clean environment. They also expect that he will be well fed and cared for.

For more information write: American Boarding Kennel

Association, 4575 Galley Rd, Suite 400, Colorado Springs, CO 80915.

PONY PICTURE PROFITS

A Lakeside, California man is making nice money by boarding both dogs and horses on his seventeen acre spread. And an innovative twist is earning him big weekend profits.

On Saturdays and Sundays this enterprising gentleman, who gave me his success story but declined to have his name put in print (something about, "I don't like to tell the world what I'm doing or how much I'm making"), runs a pony-picture operation that brings in spectacular bucks.

Recently I visited the Target store in the Magnolia Shopping Center in El Cajon, California to pick up some household items. As I was heading back to my car I saw a large smattering of people, mostly moms and kids, circled around a man and a shetland pony. I'm always curious so I went over for a look-see. Here was this dude with his little horse, raking in the cash. At $2.50 a pop he was taking pictures of kids on his horse with an old beat up Polaroid camera. Each kid was hoisted into the saddle and the photo quickly taken. "Next kid, please!"

I lit up a pipeload of fine English tobacco and decided to watch this "pony and picture" show for a while. After witnessing a dozen snapshots in less than fifteen minutes I realized he had a real moneymaker going for him. Although there was a long line of mothers with kids waiting, our tall, thin "cowboy-looking" entrepreneur decided Lady Beth (that was what he called his pony) needed a rest (hey, some of these kids weren't small!), and he fetched her a pail of water. That's when I moved in. Although he was not a talkative sort, I did learn that he boarded animals at his spread but was making much more visiting shopping centers thoughout Southern California with little Lady Beth.

I thanked him for what little information he gave me, gave

140

him a few marketing suggestions in return about having cowboy hats and toy six-guns for the kids to use when they were having their photos taken, and maybe even to sell to some of them, and let him return to business.

Obviously this is not for everyone. Most of us live in areas where we can't keep a big dog, much less a small horse. Nevertheless, for some it could be a great money-maker.

BIG BUSINESS IN BABYSITTING

No, I'm not going to tell you that you can earn big bucks as a babysitter. Frankly, most babysitters earn very little. However, there is real money to be made in operating a babysitting service. To make good money with this needed service there are three factors that can lead to success:

First, you have to have a trusted and available roster of babysitters. You can find good people by contacting your local high school or community college. Your sitters will probably have to be bonded. And you certainly ought to interview them in depth.

Secondly, you have to have a consistent supply of customers. Secure them by putting signs where parents congregate (swings, slides, teeter-totters, monkeybars, sand-boxes, baby stores, day care centers), placing regular classified ads in local papers, leaving circulars at homes in the neighborhood where babies are present or expected and purchasing a list of new parents (new being up to ten years) from a company listed in your Yellow Pages under "mailing lists." You'll be sending postcards to those parents, extolling the virtues of your babysitting service. Expect to pay about $25-$45 per 1,000 for new parents' names, plus the cost of your postcards.

Thirdly, you must handle your money collections efficiently. I recommend that you request one month payment in advance.

The rate for babysitters is no longer the 50¢ an hour you may have made when you were a kid. The range today nationwide is $1.25 to $2 per hour. To operate your sitter service profitably you should be charging 25% to 40% above the rate you pay your bevy of sitters. With a dozen or more qualified sitters, you can make substantial money. With a stable of 50 or more sitters, all kept busy most of the time, you could be earning big money.

TYPESETTING—A $100,000 A YEAR COTTAGE INDUSTRY FOR FAST FINGERS

You can set type for books, manuals, reports and magazines in your home with new photo-electronic typesetting equipment. All you need is a spare room, a relatively small investment and the ability to type. The money-making potential is awesome—from $30,000 to $100,000 per year!

A little space, fast fingers and good time management can turn a one-woman or -man Cottage Industry into a gold mine. A modern computerized photo compositor is simply a super typewriter that produces professional type in various sizes and styles on light sensitive paper. The paper is then run through a relatively small developer. Thus, an entire book can be prepared for photo-offset printing. Most typesetting machines are no larger than a small desk. This process is much faster and far more cost-effective than the now outdated traditional metal typesetting methods.

Typesetting machines sell for anywhere from $2,000 to $200,000, depending on their speed, output and variety of type. The average price for a modern machine that can handle most composition jobs is in the $20,000 to $40,000 range. While equipment buyers face a substantial investment, most manufacturers will lease equipment and accept monthly payments. Also, in a computerized field that is experiencing constant technological advancements, leasing is usually the best decision. A good service contract is another must.

While home-based typesetting can be far more lucrative than an ordinary typing service, covered previously in this manual, some forward thinking operators offer both services. Both typesetting and typing services also lend themselves to the employment of outside helpers. Although an operator would be wise to get an opinion from a tax attorney or competent accountant, several operators do use outside help on an "independent contractor" basis, thus avoiding a standard employer-employee relationship that would require various employee benefits, tax withholding, etc.

Some typesetters work closely with a free lance graphic artist, since some publishing clients and printers like to receive their type in "camera-ready" condition. The product of photo-typesetting is text strung out in long strips of paper—known in the trade as "galleys" which must be arranged with headlines and/or artwork that will eventually appear as pages.

Several typesetters find that their profit picture is brighter through specialization. Jack Lilly of Portland, Oregon has carved out a nice niche for himself in setting technical reports; Betty Brown of Boise, Idaho specializes in company newsletters and Ginger Julian of RUSH TYPE in Lakeside, California has discovered that by setting straight textual material, she can increase her volume many times over than if she were setting complicated material requiring frequent changes of type font. Marilyn Denson of Vista, California is living proof that if you are willing to handle most all types of typesetting jobs, you soon will grow beyond a one-person setup. Marilyn got started in this business in 1978 and within 5 years saw her equipment more than triple. She now also has six busy typesetters, plus a large shop, to help her keep up with the workload. Marilyn's brother Dave is an offset printer. This has worked well for both, with each referring clients to the other. It is a good idea for anyone going into the typesetting business to strike up a referral service with one or more printers in the immediate area. Some printers will send you customers, others will bill out the complete printing and typesetting package and then pay your invoice.

Many print shops like to present their customers with one billing that includes typesetting. In this way they can add 20% or more to your basic charges. Likewise, some printers will allow you commissions of 20% or more on customers you direct to them. It's one set of hands helping the other.

If typesetting sounds interesting to you as a part or full time profitable home enterprise, and there is no doubt big profits are possible, get in contact with local representatives of the leading systems in your area. These would include **COMPUGRAPHIC CORP, IBM, ADDRESSOGRAPH-MULTIGRAPH** and others.

Good used machinery is also available in most large cities from printing and office equipment brokers. Often used equipment can be bought at a fraction of the original price. However, keep in mind new technology is forever changing the state of the art, and also don't forget the importance of a service contract to avoid major expenses and "down time." In this business, "down time" means money down the drain!

Here's a company very active in buying and selling used typesetting equipment:

> Locker Typesetting Equipment
> 122 Van Houten Ave
> Passaic, NJ 07055

HOME RETAILING

Home based retailing or "Party Plan" selling as it is often referred to, is alive and well throughout the United States and Canada.

Women are still buying Tupperware, but they are also buying clothing, health products, jewelry, cosmetics, sexy lingerie and just about anything else you can buy in a retail store.

Not to be left out, many men have also gotten into the home retailing business. Many husbands and wives have joined forces to build profitable part-time or full-time home businesses.

New buying trends have many retail store owners concerned. Increased direct selling and party plan selling, often fueled by some form of multi-level marketing, is changing the buying habits of millions of consumers. Add to this the current mail order boom and it's easy to understand why retail store sales are slipping.

Tupperware now earns its parent company, Dart Industries, over 50% of its yearly profit; Mary Kay Cosmetics saw sales reach 200 million in 1982; and a southern California cosmetic/personal care product company parlayed an eighty thousand dollar investment into sales of eight million dollars in less than two years. This form of selling is hot!

Profits are available for couples or individual representatives who go with either a good established firm or a bright new shooting star. Representatives are independent contractors responsible for scheduling sales parties. $300 in sales at a party is about average for this form of selling and will bring the representative 25 to 30 percent ($75 to $90). Some representatives earn as much as 50 percent on sales, however, 25 to 30 percent is the industry average.

If you are not overly excited by these numbers, keep in mind parttime representatives often hold three or four parties per week and fulltime entrepreneurs will often hold as many as ten or more parties (some by day, others by night). Also, sharp home-based party plan retailers work constantly to improve their promotional skills to bring more people to each party. One San Diego lady, well experienced in party plan selling remarked, "If I'm not earning $25 or more for every hour I put into this, I'm not realizing my potential."

People who agree to open their homes and invite their friends and relatives in are given a nice discount on their own purchases. A small price to pay to folks who do a lot of the work for the party sales representative.

These parties not only provide "expected sales" but future parties and future sales. This is why incentives and cash bonuses are often offered to representatives who recruit other sales people.

Good money is definitely available to sales representatives, but the really big bucks go to the capable recruiter. Top recruiters who reach supervisory levels often earn $100,000 or more annually.

Home retailing is a money maker in both "good times" and "hard times". In times of economic recession, home party plans seem to continue to flourish. Perhaps because recruiting becomes easier. In difficult times more people are interested in new sources for additional income.

The boom in home retailing has attracted the attention of many power conglomerates. Colgate Palmolive now offers Princess House, Gillette has Jaffra Cosmetics and Ralston Purina has introduced Deco Plants. While it's too soon to tell if these big companies or others will have a major impact on home retailing, party plan experts have not rushed to sign up with the giants. Dan Schroeder of St. Louis Park, Minnesota, a leading recruiter in party plan selling, asks a question that no doubt is on many representatives' and recruiters' minds, "Are some big conglomerates jumping into home retailing just to grab some extra profits, or are they committed to both the people and products involved?" The answer to that question is still blowing in the wind.

Home retailing is a no overhead business with wide consumer appeal. Soft selling techniques are applied since the people at the house party are basically all friends or at least know each other. As a representative, little or no investment is required as a local distributor (sales manager) usually provides product as required. This is a people-oriented business that offers friendly, personal service. A woman (over 90% of sales representatives are female), man

146

or couple can get started for next to nothing and build a respectable income-producing business based on sales. Even larger profits, much larger, are available to the individual or couple who is successful in recruiting others to hold parties and sell products.

If you can sell products and convince others that they can do likewise, you will prosper!

PROTESTING PROFITS

Protesting is as common to America's heritage as apple pie. From a famous tea party in Boston many years ago to hunger strikes and picketing in the 1980's, the freedom to protest seems to be inbred in our citizens.

Jerry Baumburger of Detroit, Michigan noticed several auto workers picketing "unfair" hiring and layoff procedures at a local plant and the light bulb of creativity went on inside his brain. Why restrict the idea to picketing exclusively to union gripes. Many other people have plenty to protest about. Baumburger decided to start his own picketing service—a new service for people who want to complain publicly.

Two small ads; one in a local daily newspaper and another in an "alternative" weekly, got the ball rolling. Baumburger remembers his first job was picketing a used car dealer for a client who strongly felt that he had been saddled with a lemon. Baumburger had his girl friend, an art student, design an eye-catching sign. The words "don't buy here or you'll be sorry" were imposed on a large lemon, complete with wheels. Jerry was paid $50 for four hours of walking and standing in front of the dealership. "I could have made a hundred bucks," Jerry reports. "I was offered another fifty dollars by the car dealer to get my *(bleep)* away from his lot." Jerry declined of course. "In this business your loyalty belongs to the man or woman who hired you."

147

Not all picketing business is negative. Jerry Baumburger claims almost 50 percent of his picketing is positive. A local pizza parlor hires Jerry on a regular basis to tell folks *"Follow Me For the Best Pizza in Town."* A two block hike often has up to ten people in tow. Before the people enter the parlor, Jerry passes out discount coupons—50¢ off a medium size pizza, $1 off a large one. The coupons he hands out are "keyed" and although he works only on commission with the pizza shop owner, Jerry's cut—also 50¢ and $1 per customer, often brings him up to $40 in one hour.

Sherry Evans of Hollywood, California also employs pickets (paying them $5 to $10 an hour, depending on the job). She, of course, charges clients much more ($20 to $35), but for Sherry, positive or protest picketing is just a new twist to her main business—a singing telegram service.

A picket is a stiff cardboard sign, approximately 24 x 30 inches. Lettering must be neat and as few words used as possible to make the message easily readable. Attractive graphics, while not essential, certainly are desirable. This is a business that can be started on a shoestring. Anyone with a few dollars for advertising, a telephone and a willingness to be visible, can quickly be in business for himself or herself.

The laws governing picketing are not necessarily restrictive. A picket must keep moving and not block street or sidewalk traffic. The biggest negative in this businsss is the potential irate actions of a shop owner who is the object of someone's protest. A young man in Gary, Indiana was punched out by a restaurant owner who became livid when he noticed the picket sign read, *"If You Love Pets—Don't Even Let Your Dog Eat Here."* The young man was doing his own picketing after consuming "Food" at that establishment. However, the punches thrown could just as easily have decked a hired picket. Let the would-be entrepreneur beware!

Protest (or positive slogan) picketing can bring quick cash. It's a novelty-type business that could be operated parttime or fulltime from the home. The potential is there for expansion, and much larger profits would be available to the creative promoter who hustled "new accounts" while hiring others to pound the pavemment with a sign in hand.

MAKING AND REPAIRING DOLLS

One of the largest hobby groups in the United States are the "Dollers," people who collect, produce and/or repair dolls. There are hundred of thousands of "dollers" in America today and their numbers are increasing each year.

The oldest varieties of antique dolls, usually from the old world (Germany, France or Holland) are the most expensive of the group, demanding prices up to $2,000 and more apiece. One of America's all time favorites, the original Shirley Temple doll, in excellent condition, will bring $600 or more from a serious collector. While this hobby is not for poor folks, making and repairing dolls can be started with limited capital. High quality reproductions will usually sell in the $100 to $300 range. Not cheap, yet affordable for many people.

The head is of primary importance in the reproduction of a doll. Material used to cast the head is usually china, ceramic or porcelain. Plastic molds are used for casting. The ceramic is poured into a mold as a liquid. It condenses on the sides, and is removed while still damp. It is then fired in a kiln at an extremely high temperature. Lashes and eyebrows and "skin coloring" are applied prior to the final firing. Limbs can be made by the same process, however, total composition bodies—even leather bodies that are exact copies of antique bodies—may be purchased and may be combined with homemade bisque heads.

Molds are available for almost every antique doll in demand. Making your own mold is the alternative. Kiln and molds are expensive, but you need not go to this expense. You can buy "greenware" (this is unfired ceramic), do the painting yourself and hire an expert to fire it.

Sources of supplies for everything from glass eyes to heads to complete dolls can be found by subscribing to *"Doll Reader"* (published 6 times per year by Hobby House Press, Ind., 900 Frederick St., Cumberland, MD 21502 and *"Doll World"* (P.O. Box 337, Seabrook, NH 03874). The "bible" of the industry concerning pricing is the *"Blue Book of Doll Values"* by Jan Foulke (published by Hobby House Press, Inc., who also publishes "The Doll Reader").

If you would rather repair than make dolls, operating a doll hospital can be a very profitable venture. Top repair prices deal with restoring antiques. Lesser rates are usually charged for less expensive dolls. Hair must be washed regularly and curled, clothes sewn or replaced, glass eyes restored to brilliance and cracks in composition heads and bodies filled and blended in.

You need not wait to become an expert before you get started repairing dolls on a parttime basis. Novices begin by making simple repairs on popular dolls, but not antiques. Probably the most common problem is worn out elastic in the ball-joint, missing eyes and damaged hair. Sewing clothes for dolls also pays quite well. A woman in El Cajon, California figures her time at $10 profit per hour. Business is readily available from doll owners and antique dealers who wish to display a doll dressed well in order to command the highest price.

In addition to antique shop owners, get to know the folks who own doll shops in your area. These dealers may offer a repair service of their own, but are often kept so busy that they will be pleased to "farm out" extra work to you.

Another great source for doll selling and doll repairing are the many doll shows held in almost every community. You will find dates and locations of these shows in the magazines previously mentioned.

Earnings of $10 to $20 per hour are realistic for doll making. Somewhat less, $5 to $15 per hour for doll repairing. This business is definitely for a somewhat narrow audience, but if you already love dolls you can cash in on this growing hobby.

Facilities and equipment required will vary according to your own specialization. A sewing machine is important. You probably will eventually want to own your own kiln since the making of a good bisque head is the key to creating a valuable doll. Artist brushes are needed to paint skin, lips, eyelashes and brows. An air brush usually works best for very delicate cheek tints. Everything needed, including hand tools, should not cost you more than a few hundred dollars. Shop around for good used items.

SWEEPING DOWN THE PROFITS

Here's an opportunity to go into business for yourself, select your working hours, and even wear a regal top hat on the job. The profit potential? Very high! The investment? Moderate. About $2,500 or less! The demand? Rapidly increasing!

Tommy Lee Pelcher in Baton Rouge, LA pockets a tidy $250 for 8 hours work, and Edward Stillman of Austin, TX demands—and gets—$400 for the same amount of time. What does Tommy Lee, Edward and hundreds of other innovative businessmen (it seems that this field is dominated by men but there are couples too who work together) do for the nice bucks they receive? They are chimney sweeps!

Sweeping chimneys may not be your idea of having a good time, but...

The work really isn't that bad and the pay is excellent. Parttimers generally clean two or three an evening plus four or five more on weekends. Most "sweeps" now charge $50 for cleaning the first chimney and $35 or $40 for each additional one on each job.

151

Why will people "being of sound mind" pay some strange character in a black suit and top hat fifty bucks or more to clean up a chimney? Safety is your answer!

When solid fuels (wood, coal, etc.) are burned in a stove, furnace or fireplace, soot and creosote build up. Unless a chimney is cleaned regularly, flammable soot and creosote will accumulate in the flue. This can drastically weaken a chimney. If left uncleaned for a long time, the results can be destructive. A home owner can eventually lose the entire chimney. Worse yet, unwanted fire in the chimney could ignite a blaze that turns the whole house into an inferno.

Soon after *World War II*, America and Canada switched almost completely from solid fuel to more convenient oil, gas and electricity. It appeared the day of wood and coal burning heat was over forever. But alas, history has a way of repeating itself. The "energy crisis" of the seventies abruptly sent millions of people into at least supplemental heating of their homes with wood and coal.

Electricity, oil and gas may be "cleaner" and more "convenient" than wood or coal but they are also a lot more expensive. The entire nation may not be ready to return to the heating method used by their parents or grandparents, but several million are starting a trend in that direction. This means thousands of more chimney sweeps will be in big demand. The real risk of a devastating fire in solid heated homes makes this service a necessity.

TOP HAT AND TAIL
FOR A POSITIVE IMAGE

Any chimney sweep worth his salt will wear the proud and ancient European garb of "black hat and tails." Modern-day opportunists tell me this also pays off with a highly visible image that is easily recognizable. Free publicity in local newspapers and magazines or on radio or television seems to

152

come easy for the "fully dressed" sweeps. This can really give the new home-based biz a big send off.

THE JOB ITSELF

Chimney sweeps knock loose and scrub out every particle of soot and creosote that can be removed from the flue. How best is this done? Ask ten sweeps this question and you'll get ten different answers. Some sweeps recommend round brushes, others insist the square ones are better. Some like hard brushes, others prefer the soft ones. Some say you sweep from the bottom up, others snicker and say a good sweep starts atop the roof. All good chimney sweeps get the job done right, but they certainly have many different means to reach the same end.

Sweeping chimneys may not be your idea of having a good time, but it sure can be profitable. $500 to $1,000 a week is a realistic goal for fulltime work and parttimers are reporting earnings in the $200 to $700 range. We've even heard an unsubstantiated report out of Columbus, Ohio of a young man who, along with his wife and brother, started sweeping chimneys in 1983 and earned a ten thousand dollar profit—split between them—their first month. This seems a mite high, but the possibilities in this new (old) business are truly remarkable.

Once you own the "tools of the trade," and you do need specialized tools, you are ready to advertise. Use newspapers and local shoppers. Also go after free publicity in any and all local media. Another source of jobs can be a little ad in real estate publications in your area. Realtors also can be a good source of referrals.

Although you can get started on your own, and on a shoestring, you may wish to look into the very low priced franchise opportunity being offered by the Chimney Sweep, Inc., Rt. 8, Box 36, NE, Rome, GA 30161.

FOSSIL FINDING
HAVING FUN—AND MAKING MONEY

Rocks contain a great deal of history. They also offer unusual profit potential in the form of fossils.

Fossils can be the petrified remains or impressions of entire humans or animals or of their bony parts, skin, features, or tracks, or any telltale evidence of the presence or passing of creatures from the past.

Among the most valuable to collectors and museums are the trilobites. They roamed the world's oceans some 500 million years ago, and ranged in size from about one inch to 18 inches or more. Though the trilobites haven't been with us for millions of years, their fossilized remains are commonly found all over the country.

Also quite popular and not too hard to find, are the ceohalopod—a shelled forefather of the octopus and squid—that lived in Missouri some 350 to 400 million years ago.

WHERE TO LOOK? Fossils can be found everywhere— every hillside, quarry and water bed is a potential "finding grounds." Even the rocks in your field or home garden can contain rare specimens. However, the more you know about fossils and the geological formations where they are likely to be found, the more treasures you'll be able to locate.

The best place to find fossils is where you find sedimentary rock that was laid down under a prehistoric body of water and is characteristically layered. Many of the creatures that once lived in and near the pond, lake or sea will be preserved within the solidified sediment. This is especially true if they had hard parts on their bodies such as carapaces, shells or bones. The creatures' remains will have survived the millions of years since their demise as impressions (casts or molds). Sometimes they will be partially or completely "replaced" by dissolved minerals. Since organic matter disintegrates very slowly, these replacements can sometimes create an exact replica in stone. Even down to the cellular level.

The fossil finder will sometimes find specimens "weatherered out" on the exterior of rocks. Usually, however, it is necessary to split the strata in your search. Tightly embedded specimens must, of course, be extracted with extreme care.

Always keep in mind the discovery of one preserved organism will suggest that others could be nearby. Remember, too, that fossils are almost always close to what once was the creature's natural habitat.

TOP FIND! Following are the more popular fossils among the commonly found varieties.

Trilobites look like chubby insects and are usually 1½ to 4 inches long. Their heads (cephalons), segmented bodies (thoraxes) and tails (pygidia) are often discovered separately since these creatures would shed their shells to accommodate growth much as crustaceans (lobsters, crabs, etc.) do today. Complete specimens are highly prized.

Cephalopods have big cylindrical shells. This group includes nautiloids, ammonites, and straight cephalopods. They often have intricate and ornate ridges and markings. The shells can range from a couple of inches to several feet in diameter or length.

Crinoids are delicate flowerlike sea creatures that have heads, arms and stems. Finding stem sections are quite common and of very little value to the serious collector. Intact they bring a decent price.

Other fossils include fish skeletons, insects, animal and bird tracts, sharks teeth and petrified wood, among others.

REWARDS: Payment for trilobites can be as little as $5 or less or as much as $400 for a "perfect" specimen. The same is true of cephalopods. Some shells are so common as to be virtually valueless but an unusual specimen will always find a buyer. Crinoids, when whole and intact, command a price of $40 to $100.

If my description of various fossils mentioned here, including how to find them and profit from them, have you stimulated but still somewhat uncertain, you'll need to start digging for more information.

An excellent book for beginners is *The Weekend Fossil Hunter* by Jerry D. La Plante. Mr. La Plante's book is filled with helpful information on rock identification, tools needed, map study and fossil extraction. It also lists the very best fossil areas in all states. Published by Drake Publishers, Inc., it is available in most rock shops.

The "bible" of the industry is *Index Fossils of North America* by Harvey W. Shimer and Robert R. Shrock (M.I.T. Press). This monumental reference guide is available at many libraries.

HOW TO START AN
ENTREPRENEUR'S CLUB
IN YOUR CITY

There are Elks Clubs, Press Clubs, Toastmaster Clubs and 1001 other clubs found in cities across the nation. Why not start a new club for business people and entrepreneurs in your city. The trend has already started in many California cities. Some have started as non-profit organizations, others are strictly for the profit of all concerned, including the promoter.

While it is too soon to tell if existing clubs are operating profitably, I see great potential and you can get started on a shoestring.

Here's the plan. In a mid-size or major city (I don't think prospects would be good in a small town), make inquiries with local hotels concerning a free meeting room (hall) in exchange for their serving lunch to everyone who attends. Select the establishment which offers the nicest facilities and the best price for a simple but good lunch. A promoter in Columbus (a mid-size town) told us he averages 100 people at the hotel, provides the room and caters the meal for $6 per person. Since the promoter charges each "member" $12, he doubles his money, less expenses.

Your only expenses are related to building attendance. Go for all the free publicity you can get (television, radio, newspapers). Also you can get your cause a real boost by seeking speaking engagements before business-oriented groups (Chamber of Commerce, neighborhood business organizations, etc.). Tell everyone your story: You are launching a business/entrepreneur club for everyone in business for himself or herself, or anyone hoping to start a business—any kind of business. You will meet regularly (once a month on a weekday) and provide an interesting speaker, lunch and an attractive setting for people to mingle and exchange ideas. All for a reasonable amount (keep your charge in the $10 to $15 range).

If you make a dedicated effort to obtain publicity you should get plenty with this novel promotion. The more publicity, the more people who will attend. Lots of people in business will realize the importance of attending, even more who want to start a business will recognize the opportunity.

On a parttime basis, working only a few hours a month, you can drum up some good money with this promotion. And the service you provide is terrific. All sorts of good and highly interesting things happen when a bunch of entrepreneurs get together to hear a good speech, break bread and talk business with one another.

A keynote speaker at your meetings is a must. By massaging an ego or giving a man or woman with a hot new product a chance to address an eager audience, you can often land a great speaker for peanuts, or even scott free! It will be important to pay very little, if anything, to your speakers during your first few formative months. Later you may decide it is wise to pay a good fee to land a great speaker who can help build your audience.

You can go on a month-to-month basis, allowing folks to reserve by phone a day or two before the meetings, or even walk in without reservations. Just make sure you know your hotel's policy. Some hotels are pretty flexible, others want to know how many they will be serving in advance. The more flexible your hotel and its catering arrangement the better!

Have all guests sign a book that will give you a valuable mailing list. A postcard reminder a week or so before each meeting will help these folks become repeaters.

Later, after you firmly establish your club, you may want to sell yearly "memberships". For example, by subscription a person could be allowed to attend 12 meetings, complete with lunch, for the normal price of ten. Since business folks do travel quite a bit, you could issue "tickets" and allow your "member" to give them to others to use, if she or he chooses.

One more vital point. In operating any kind of club it is very important to maintain the same date, time and place. Example: "the last Friday of each month, 12 o'clock noon at the Ramada Inn." Friday is your best choice of days since many people will have lunch, listen to your speaker, rap with fellow members for a while and then go home early. Saturdays are great for seminars (workshops) for many people, but not for the self-employed. They prefer weekday meetings.

Starting a business meeting club in your city could mean good business for you. Perhaps, just as important, it would help establish you as a business leader in your community. Think about all the great contacts you'll meet! You'll be on a one-to-one, first name basis with many of these movers, shakers and money makers (say, that's not too bad a name for a business entrepreneur club) in your area.

HOME BUSINESS FRANCHISES

While most people who start their own home, or home-based business, do so from square one, there are now dozens and dozens of excellent franchise business opportunities that I wish to present here for your consideration.

Obviously, there are pros and cons to both (starting on your own or becoming a part of a larger, established organization). However, it's good to consider all of your options.

BUSINESS FRANCHISES

Business support systems are big business today. If you're already office smart, or willing to learn (night adult education courses abound today) one of these opportunities could mean big biz for you!

GENERAL BUSINESS
SERVICES
51 Monroe St.
Rockville, MD 20850
Product/Service: Accounting services, business and management consulting.
Minimum franchise fee: $18,500
Total capital required: $21,500
Royalty: 7%

FYC FILE YOUR CLAIMS
401 E. Parker St.
Pinckneyville, IL 62274
Product/Service: Filling out forms, doing paperwork, typing for clients.
Minimum franchise fee: Under $12,000
Total capital required: Up to $28,000
Royalty: 5%

159

COMPREHENSIVE
BUSINESS/ACCOUNTING
SERVICES
2111 Comprehensive Dr.
Aurora, IL 60570
Product/Service: Bookkeeping,
accounting, income tax and
management services.
Minimum franchise fee: $68
Total capital required: $25,000
and up
Royalty: 12.5%
Financing help available

BUTLER LEARNING
SYSTEMS
1325 Dorothy Lane
Dayton, OH 45409
Product/Service: Programs and
seminars for professionals, or-
ganizations
Minimum franchise fee: Under
$10,000
Total capital required: $10,000
and up
Royalty: 10%

SYSTEM VII
14110 East Firestone Blvd.
Santa Fe Springs, CA 90670
Product/Service: Insurance
sales and service.
Minimum franchise fee: $799
Total capital required: $1,000 to
$2,000
Royalty: 10%
Financing help available

HEALTH, FITNESS AND BEAUTY

Since the dawn of time, people have wanted to look better
and feel better. These opportunities take aim at the huge,
and ever-expanding better health, fitness and vanity marketplace.

JAZZERCISE
2808 Roosevelt St.
Carlsbad, CA 92008
Product/Service: Dance fitness
programs
Minimum franchise fee: $500
Total capital required: Less
than $10,000
Royalty: 10%

ALOETTE
341 Lancaster Ave.
Malvern, PA 79355
Product/Service: Home show
cosmetic sales
Minimum franchise fee: $5,000
Total capital required: $9,000
Royalty: 0
Financing help available

PROFESSIONAL WAY
CORPORATION
27173 Grand River
Detroit, MI 48240
Product/Service: Consumable dental products marketed to dental professionals
Minimum franchise fee: $10,000 or less
Total capital required: Variable
Royalty: Unknown

PARCOURSE FITNESS
CIRCUITS/CLUSTERS/
MODULES
443 Tehama St.
San Francisco, CA 94103
Product/Service: Sell and install self-guiding fitness courses
Minimum franchise fee: $2,000 to $4,000
Total capital required: $4,000 to $12,000
Royalty: Unknown

SLENDER CENTER, INC.
1245 Washington Ave.
Madison, WI 53521
Product/Service: Weight loss consultation service
Minimum franchise fee: $8,000 to $23,000
Total capital required: $10,000 to $28,000
Royalty: Annually, $2,000 minimum

SONDANCE, INC.
P.O. Box 458
Royal Oak, MI 48068
Product/Service: Dance, fitness, incorporating posture, mental fitness
Minimum franchise fee: $100 to $500
Total capital required: $1,000 to $5,000
Royalty: Negotiable

STOP SMOKING CENTERS
11504 Prendergast
St. Louis, MO 63138
Royalty: Stop-smoking program, medically referred
Minimum franchise fee: $9,900
Total capital required:$15,000
Royalty: Unknown

TAKE TIME
1515 East Silver Springs Blvd.
Ocala, FL 32670
Product/Service: Exercise instruction
Minimum franchise fee: $10,000
Total capital required: $10,000 to $75,000
Royalty: 5%

HOUSEHOLD AND LIGHT CLEANING AND COMMERCIAL AND HEAVY DUTY FRANCHISES

POP-INS, INC.
1 West Park Ave.
Columbiana, OH 44408
Product/Service: Home, condo, office, apartment cleaning
Minimum franchise fee: $9,500
Total capital required: $18,000
Royalty: 7½%

MAID BRIGADE SERVICES
850 Indian Trail
Atlanta, GA 30247
Product/Service: Maid service
Minimum franchise fee: Below $10,000
Total capital required:$12,000 plus
Royalty: 6%

SUNSHINE POLISHING SYSTEMS
1551 Camino del Rio, S., #218
San Diego, CA 92108
Product/Service: Mobile car, truck, boat polishing
Minimum franchise fee: $875
Total capital required:$2,500
Royalty: Varies

CHEM-DRY CARPET CLEANING
3300 Cameron Park Dr.
Cameron Park, CA 95682
Product/Service: Carpet cleaning
Minimum franchise fee: $5,200
Total capital required: $4,750
Royalty: $43.08 per month
Financing help available

SERVICEMASTER
2300 Warrenville Road
Downers Grove, IL 60515
Product/Service: Carpet, window, drapery and wall cleaning
Minimum franchise fee: $9,750
Total capital required: Up to $10,000
Royalty: 7-10%
Financing help available

RAINBOW INTERNATIONAL CARPET DYEING AND CLEANING
1010 University Parks Dr.
Waco, TX 76707
Product/Service: Carpet, upholstery and drapery cleaning and dyeing
Minimum franchise fee: $15,000
Total capital required: $10,000
Royalty: 7%

SPARKLE WASH
26851 Richmond Road
Beford Heights, OH 44146
Product/Service: Mobile power cleaning service
Minimum franchise fee: $20,000
Total capital required: $45,000
Royalty: 3%
Financing help available

DURACLEAN, INTL.
2151 Waukegan Road
Deerfield, IL 60015
Product/Service: Carpet, furniture and drapery cleaning service
Minimum franchise fee: Varies
Total capital required: $19,800
Royalty: Variable
Financing help available

SERVPRO
11357 Pyrites Way
Rancho Cordova, CA 95670
Product/Service: Office and residential cleaning services
Minimum franchise fee: $33,000
Total capital required: Up to $75,000
Royalty: 7-10%
Financing help available

MINI MAID SERVICES, INC.
747 Chance Road
Marietta, GA 30066
Product/Service: Residential carpet and window cleaning
Minimum franchise fee: $7,900
Total capital required: $15,000
Royalty: $250 per month

REPAIR AND MAINTENANCE FRANCHISES

Did you ever know a "handyman" who did not make money in good times or bad times? Repair and maintenance are big biz today, and these firms could help you reap the rich rewards available.

MR. BUILD
2114 N. Broadway
Santa Ana, CA 92706
Product/Service: Commercial and home construction and repair
Minimum franchise fee: $4,000
Total capital required: Up to $10,000
Royalty: About $650 per month
Financing help available

PERMA CERAM ENTERPRISES
65 Smithtown Rd.
Smithtown, NY 11787
Product/Service: Bathroom resurfacing
Minimum franchise fee: $14,500
Total capital required: Up to $10,000
Royalty: 0

DECORATING DEN
SYSTEMS, INC.
4630 Montgomery Ave.
Bethesda, MD 20814
Product/Service: Home decorating products; custom draperies, carpet, wallcovering, furniture
Minimum franchise fee: $15,000
Total capital required: $25,000
Royalty: 11%
Financing help available

ALMOST HEAVEN
HOT TUBS
Route 5FF
Renick, WV 24966
Product/Service: Hot tubs, spas, whirlpools and saunas
Minimum franchise fee: 0
Total capital required: $10,000
Royalty: 0

LADIES IN PAINTING, INC.
640 E. Grant St.
Minneapolis, MN 55404
Product/Service: Interior painting/contracting
Minimum franchise fee: $4,000
Total capital required: $15,000
Royalty: 10%

LIK-NU PORCELAIN, INC
179 Woodbury Rd.
Hicksville, NY 11801
Product/Service: Porcelain refinishing and repair
Minimum franchise fee: Under $10,000
Total capital required: Varies
Royalty: Varies

MIRACLE METHOD, INC.
1280 Monument Blvd.
Concord, CA 94520
Product/Service: Porcelain refinish and repair
Minimum franchise fee: $10,000
Total capital required: $20,000
Royalty: 7½%

L&M LAWNCARE, INC.
12661 Chillicothe Road
Chesterfield, OH 44026
Product/Service: Patented fertilizer, plus insecticide and herbicide spraying, commercial and residential
Minimum franchise fee: $9,500
Total capital required: $20,000 to $50,000
Royalty: 8%

HOUSEMASTER OF
AMERICA
421 West Union Ave.
Bound Brook, NH 08805
Product/Service: Home inspection for buyers
Minimum franchise fee: $12,000
Total capital required: $22,000 to $34,000
Royalty: 6%

MR. ROOTER
4100 Will Rogers Pkwy., #100
Oklahoma City, OK 73108
Product/Service: Sewer and drain cleaning
Minimum franchise fee: $12,500
Total capital required: $12,500 and up
Royalty: 6% per week

164

BATH GENIE
109 E. Main St.
Marlboro, MA 017524
Product/Service: Bathtub re-
surfacing
Minimum franchise fee: 0
Total capital required: $20,000
Royalty: 0

LINDAL CEDAR
HOMES, INC.
4300 S. 104th Pl.
Seattle, WA 98124
Product/Service: Pre-cut cedar
homes
Minimum franchise fee: $5,000
Total capital required: $40,000
to $100,000

DIAL ONE
INTERNATIONAL
4100 Long Beach Blvd.
Long Beach, CA 90807
Product/Service: Property
maintenance and repair services
Minimum franchise fee: $2,300
to $5,000
Total capital required: Up to
$10,000
Royalty: Variable

That concludes this rich buffet of home business opportunities. I hope one or more (there is nothing to keep you from launching more than one profit-project at the same time) is just right for you.

Perhaps, even more important than any specific opportunity presented here, is the awakening process that comes within. Do you feel those *Creative juices* beginning to stir? You do? Good! Keep them flowing! Trust in yourself and your God-given abilities. ***Think. Plan. Act.*** If you want to ***Stay Home And Make Money***, YOU CAN DO IT!

SECTION THREE:

Writing
and/or
Self-Publishing
Success

Writing and/or self-publishing for profits is a great home business. Perhaps there is a better way to get paid for creative self-expression, but if there is, it's a mystery to me.

I have helped thousands of writers and independent information publishers, and mail order booksellers, get started in this exciting and lucrative field, many of whom have gone forward to smashing success. If this field is attractive to you, the information in this section of *Stay Home and Make Money,* can fling open the door to a bright new future for you.

This information was written for any man or woman, with or without previous writing experience, who wants to make money—a little extra money—or lots of long green, through the process I call: *writing, publishing and selling words.*

Don't let "professor-type experts" trick you into thinking you need a long literary background to succeed.

Here are the only 5 qualities you *do* need to succeed in information writing/publishing.

(1) Knowledge on how to get started right

(2) A positive mental attitude and great desire

(3) Knowledge that you have or will obtain to share with others

(4) A marketing strategy

(5) Great persistence

If you will supply the positive mental attitude, and the perseverance, I'm going to help you find the right topic for you (if it isn't already known to you), plus give you good start-up knowledge and proven marketing ideas and techniques.

For best results, I recommend you zero in on a "how to" or information topics. Leave fiction, poetry, autobiographies, etc., to those few writers who are making money with it, and to the tens of thousands who would like to crack this small marketplace, but usually fall short.

WRITING

FINDING SUBJECTS
TO WRITE ABOUT

A work of fiction must be brought forth from deep within the author's being. To be successful, it must reek with originality. Good, solid, nonfiction works must also be spiced with creativity; however, here the author relies heavily upon research and/or past experiences to produce a strong manuscript.

Information subject matter for articles, fillers, reports, booklets or full-size books can be found anywhere and everywhere. For the very best results start with your own field of expertise or one you wish to read about and research. Don't kid me or yourself. If you're an adult who has not led a very secluded life, you have useful information on a subject or subjects that folks will pay you to learn.

Focus on providing people with simple, understandable, and helpful information that will satisfy any of their basic "WANTS AND NEEDS," and your work can become a BEST SELLER. More importantly, you will make money and also feel good about it. A double pay off!

169

Here is a partial list of what interests readers (people):

People Want To Be:	People Want To Have	People Want To Do
Loved	More money	Their own thing
Appreciated	Advancement in business	Start their own business
Admired	Security for the future	Express their individuality
Beautiful	More leisure time	Accomplish something
Creative	Improved health	important
Powerful	Self-esteem	Obtain affection and love
Respected	Peace of mind	Important tasks
Productive	Self-control	Improve themselves
Informed	Pleasure	Travel to exciting places
Free	Improved physical	Have more fun
Successful	appearance	Do less work
Recognized	More personal prestige	Make a greater
Forgiven	More creature comforts	contribution

As both a writer/publisher and marketing consultant, I never cease to be amazed at the huge number of folks who have valuable information between their ears and don't consider packaging and selling it. Some just keep giving it away free, or much worse, they keep it to themselves.

This is the age of specialized information. People are ready, willing and able to pay good money for zillions of different forms of useful knowledge. Simply find a need and fill it. And needs are found everywhere. From spiritual bliss to how to have a successful garage sale, and from a super new diet to how to bake a better apple pie to improving your sexual performance—the list of topics is eternal. Never fear, you will never run out of available and saleable words to sell.

Here's a meaningful exercise. Grab yourself paper and pen and write down every subject you have some degree of knowledge about. Don't bother putting these subject headings in any order of importance. Just jot them down as they drop down from your mind. After several minutes, when you begin groping for more headings, stop. Now examine your list and pick the topics that most interest you and get busy writing!

170

FINDING THE TIME TO WRITE

"I just don't find time to write." The No. 1 copout of all would-be authors. Your success depends on effective use of time!

You have heard the time-tested saying, "If you want something done, ask a busy person to do it." Busy, productive people who effectively manage their time will somehow get things done and meet their goals. At the same time the person who doesn't manage time will sit at the desk and stare at the work that should be done. Or perhaps shuffle papers without accomplishing anything or quite likely, make excuses not to start at all.

Misuse of time seldom involves an isolated incident; it almost always is part and parcel of a well-established pattern of poor work habits. God knows, changing or reprogramming our behavior is not an easy task. Learning to cope with the clock and make it work for us rather than against us is no simple behavior change. The potential pay-off is so beneficial however, that we must turn destructive, time-wasting habits into rewarding habits that best utilize the precious gift that is time.

DOWN WITH CLUTTER

Many business people in general, and writers in particular, have huge piles of papers, envelopes and current work on their desks, somehow assuming the more important matters, like cream, will rise to the top.

For rare individuals some clutter actually seems to work. Since clutter has often been a part of my own experience, I have often rationalized it. "I'd go nuts if I had to maintain a tidy desk," is my plea to anyone who will listen. However, after getting serious about effective time management, I no longer can justify all my clutter and "piles." My desk is still never really neat and some clutter prevails; however, I have come a long way. I intend to continue to improve in this vital area and I strongly suggest you do likewise. I don't want to preach perfection, mind you, I just want all of us to avoid that chaotic, sinking feeling. Clutter can create tension and frustration; it can make us feel "hopelessly snowed under." That feeling can lead to unproductive work or escape. When a writer gets frustrated his work will be sub-par, if that person works at all. A work bottleneck is often followed by the mind shutting down. This is the "mental block" ploy that writers too often accept as an uncontrollable occurrence thus giving it power in their experience. Is is both avoidable and controllable. One excellent method to prevent the mental block syndrome is to keep both your desk and your mind free from clutter.

An effective means of dealing with your papers, projects, mail, etc., is to go through them and divide them into five categories:

(1) High Priority—Immediate Action
(2) Low Priority
(3) Pending
(4) Reading Matter
(5) Wastebasket

Put all high priority items on top of your desk. Put all other items out of sight. Put them in your desk, under your desk or on a side table, in any case out of sight! (Naturally, all items in category five are already off your desk and in the circular file. Excellent time managers make liberal use of the wastebasket.)

Now sort through your high priority items and choose the one that ranks No. 1 in importance and have at it. Don't go on to anything else until this is accomplished, and so on and so on. When all top priority matters have been handled, pull up the stack of low priority items and work on them.

YOUR WRITING TIMETABLE

One more crucial thought on your "high priority" list. Set aside a time to work exclusively on your current topic. It doesn't matter what particular writing task you are working on. What is important is that you set aside a certain period of time daily to accomplish it. If you can only spend two hours daily on our new "word selling business," at least spend those 2 hours wisely. Perhaps one hour will have to be spent on the business aspects of writing. Set up a work schedule employing the five categories given. This would leave you with one hour daily (perhaps much more on weekends) to work on your chosen subject. For best results hold fast to this timetable and make it a daily routine. It is generally best to use the same work time each time (some writers do their best work very early in the mornings, others keep a pot of coffee brewing as they work in the wee hours of night). Find your best time and then stick with it. Most pros who write for a living (your ultimate goal?) keep a rigid schedule. My own "time to write" is both early and late. I have discovered 8 a.m. till 11 a.m. are three good morning hours for me, as are the late evening hours of 10 p.m. till around midnight. My concentration ebbs during "day time hours" and I use my time with routine business activities.

PRIVACY IS A MUST

You need a time to write and you also need a place to write. If you already have an office in your home or a spare bedroom to turn into one, you have it made. If no such luxury exists, see if room exists in your garage—if it has adequate lighting, heat, etc. If all else fails, use your own bedroom evenings and put it off limits to other family members for that hour or two in which you put words on paper. Some Word Sellers may set up shop on the kitchen table nights, but I have always felt the interruption factor there makes this household center a poor work area.

The kitchen table, for a start, is okay as a mail processing area if your writing is being marketed by mail order—in which case, family members are not "off limits." Their help is strongly solicited and will be much appreciated. You may even consider letting "Sonny" use the family car Saturday night if he licks enough stamps and stuffs enough envelopes, etc. How you bribe your spouse is your own concern. By now, you should know how to *push the right buttons.*

Single people make fine writers. They also can conduct successful mail order businesses. The only thing they lack that a married person has (or should I say *may have*) is built-in cheap labor. The single person must either (1) do it himself or herself or (2) hire outside help.

In all fairness there are advantages and disadvantages in both cases. Sure your spouse and children love you, still a favor rendered means favors sought in return. Just think about all the trouble that boy might get into with your car Saturday night. On second thought, don't think about it!

STOP PROCRASTINATION— TAKE ACTION *NOW!*

The "I'll do that later" mentality prevents a multitude of great accomplishments. It robs you of time, money and true success. If procrastination is your problem, don't put off doing something about it!

The fundamental reason most people procrastinate is because they have formed a habit of avoiding responsibility. Again we must be willing to change old unproductive habits. For the writer, here are three solid suggestions:

(1) Decide to change—starting NOW! Starting today (not tomorrow) set aside your time to write and handle related business matters.

(2) To find the necessary hours in a week for putting words on paper, willingly make the sacrifice. In many cases, simply cutting out or cutting down on TV viewing (a major enemy

of your Creative Force) will produce all the time you require to allow yourself to write for money.

(3) Don't give up. Too many people quit when they are drawing near a smashing success. Don't give up on yourself. You can do it! Also, if you find yourself slipping backward into old procrastinating habits, recognize your backsliding and take charge of your life. At first it may be two steps forward and one backward. If you continue to reinforce positive new success habits, you'll soon take ten strides forward for every tiny step back.

DON'T LET OTHERS WASTE YOUR TIME

Since most of us are masters at wasting our own time, we damn sure don't want outside help. You owe a certain amount of time to your family and friends. Strong marriages and true friendships require time and effort. Just remember, it was actually your own fault. You *let* them take your time.

YOUR TIME IS NOW

Effective time management is of paramount importance to all success-minded people. For writers it is absolutely essential. I trust the time I have spent on this subject has not been in vain. By taking charge of the time in your life, you'll soon be enjoying the time of your life! Guaranteed!

PROFIT FROM MAGAZINE ARTICLES

The late 1970s saw a publishing explosion of magazines in America. Readers soon saw many new titles compete for public interest. Today, as we approach the 1990s, there is a magazine published on every conceivable subject—usually several magazines on *every* topic. In some areas it has become a little ridiculous (the men's—or sex—magazine field, for example). Today, no less than 300 different sexy mags are being published monthly, bimonthly or quarterly. Now that's a lot of words and bare flesh competing for reader and viewer interest. For the sophisticated adult article writer, it is also a vast paying market for free-lance talent. Not every *word seller* can crack the biggies like *Playboy, Penthouse, Oui,* etc., but some of the second-stringers like *Fling, Dude* and *Cavalier,* also pay cash money for articles, short stories, etc.

Maybe all these crazy *skin mags* aren't your cup of tea, but how about earning nice checks from several of the thousands of other national, regional and trade magazines that are open to free-lance submissions? You have a wide open market available to you and unlimited topics.

START IN THE MIDDLE OF THE HEAP AND WORK UP

When it comes to submitting articles to magazines, most new writers aim too high or too low. As an unknown typewriter tickler or pencil pusher, who hired a typist to neatly arrange words on paper, you have a chance to have your articles published in leading national magazines such as *Reader's Digest, Cosmopolitan,* or *Playboy.* Your chances, however, are just slightly better than your chance to win the Irish Sweepstakes. Sure, it's possible, but the odds are mighty long. Wait till you build a solid reputation before hunting the big game.

While one group of novice writers address their manila envelopes to the biggest and most widely read national magazines, the other group sends off their manuscripts to only those little local magazines who offer small pay or no pay to their hapless contributors. Some say, get your feet wet. Get your work in print, at any cost (even no pay!). Yours truly disregards this thinking, and I wish to emphasize, you trade your words for financial consideration, and nothing else. Unless, of course, you wish to donate writing talent to your favorite club, charity or other non-profit organization. I have much more respect for those who keep getting rejected by aiming their articles at the heavyweight national magazines, than the person who writes articles just to see his or her name in print. The best route to steady flow of cash for your articles is to get started with middle-pack publications who can't pay the big loot but who do offer reasonable pay for accepted submissions. This great *secondary market* is an excellent media for breaking into print for a profit!

WHAT THE EDITORS WANT

After reading many market reports and writers guidelines supplied by hundreds of magazines, I'm convinced *human interest* is the numero uno magazine article success factor, followed closely by *self-help, personality profiles* and *personal experiences.*

Even pragmatic business and trade journals want human interest interwoven in the success stories they print. Today's article writer must learn to write about real people while passing on information.

HUMAN INTEREST ARTICLES

Since fact can really be more exciting than fiction, readers want to feel the human drama in your informative writing. People never tire of success stories of men and women who started at the bottom (or battled much adversity) and rose to the top of the heap! You will never miss if you work on still another rags-to-riches true experience—yours or someone else's.

SELF-HELP AND "HOW-TO" ARTICLES

There is no end to the public appetite for good "how-to" and "self-help" articles on a thousand different topics. To crack this lucrative market you need only share your own true experiences or visit your library to research topics that interest you. You can also tie these articles into a self-publishing book effort. Many a shrewd article writer has expanded his article(s) into a report, booklet or full-size self-published book and enjoyed resounding success. On the flip side of the money wheel, many a sharp self-publisher has raked in nice "extra profits" by spin off articles from a previously published book.

PERSONAL EXPERIENCES

All but the most withdrawn and secluded among us are constantly encountering experiences that can bring us recognition and reimbursement when shared in print. The outstanding feature of sharing life's personal experiences, is that we have lived them and are best suited to present them to our readers. Don't think that personal experiences must be momentous to be saleable to magazine editors. They need only be original, stimulating, creative and chock-full of human interest. True, a stranger-than-fiction story of how

178

you once lived in a haunted house filled with ghosts will spark high interest in many people, but some other folks will be just as interested in your childhood reflections on the coldest winter in St. Paul, Minnesota or the hottest summer in Tucson, Arizona. Or any one of a zillion other engrossing personal encounters.

Since experiences are on-going and because life tosses us many curves, change-ups and sliders along with the hard fastballs, the alert and reflective *word seller* never need lack personal experience subject matter. The world outside is filled with new happenings, personal contacts, and constant human drama. Then too, the inner world is forever creative. Let your ideas, thoughts, reflections, mind patterns and dreams be your guide. For it is in the *windmills of your mind* that the seeds of great new articles are ready to grow, bloom and be richly harvested.

MARKETING ARTICLES

Just as the self-publisher must *keep on keeping on* after writing his or her book, booklet or report, the article writer must keep revising and soliciting magazine editors until his piece has been accepted. A series of rejections must not intimidate the writer, though they may make the author consider a new rewrite, with perhaps a slightly different twist.

There are magazines and trade journals for *every* type of conceivable article or filler that you may wish to write. Two of the most comprehensive marketing books every *word seller* should own are:

Writer's Market, $14.95 plus $1.00 postage/handling from *Writer's Digest Books*, P.O. Box 42261, Cincinnati, OH 45242 and

The Writer's Handbook, also $14.95 plus $1.00 postage/ handling from *The Writer, Inc.*, 8 Arlington St., Boston, Mass. 02116.

179

Both will be found in your local library, but as reference works, they canot be checked out. I recommend ownership. Check for them in your favorite local bookstore, or order by mail. Another book very helpful to the article writer that I highly recommend is:

MAGAZINE WRITING—The Inside Angle, $10.95 plus $2.00 postage/handling from *Writer's Digest Books,* P.O. Box 42261, Cincinnati, OH 45242.

There is money to be made—lots of it!—writing magazine articles. I use article writing to help promote my self-published books and for "extra income." Many writers earn steady income selling words to magazines exclusively. In either case, magazine article writing deserves your consideration. It is a wide-open marketplace and very responsive. Go for it!

WHAT'S IT WORTH?

Although most conventional publishers of books, magazines, or journals spell out clearly the fees they will render to their writers, dozens and dozens of other kinds of free lance jobs have no set fees. Each writer must determine his or her own worth.

Listed here are a collection of jobs requiring free lance input and rough fee guidelines for same. I realize many of my *Words for Wealth* will demand higher pay for their writing skills, while others may choose to render their service for less money. That's each writer's own personal decision. Perhaps based on one's current workload, time availability, or a desire to eat regularly. The following jobs and rates will serve as a helpful guide.

Advertising. Very subjective, depending on type of work. My examples: Full page ad in national magazine, $750; ½ page ad, $450; 1 col. inch, $60. In local publications, full page ad, $500; ½ page ad, $300; 1 col. inch, $40.

Associations, writing for, on miscellaneous projects: $10 to $25 per hour or on a project basis.

As-told-to books. Author gets full advance and 50% royalties; subject gets 50% royalties.

Audio cassette scripts. $1,000 to $1,500 advance against 6 to 10% royalties for 5 to 10 script/visual units.

Biography, writing for a sponsor. $500 and up to $3,000 plus expenses over a two-year period.

Book manuscript copy editing. $5 to $8 per hour.

Book manuscript rewriting. $1,000 and up; $400 per day and up.

Book manuscript typing: $1 to $1.75 per double-spaced page.

Booklets, writing and editing. $500 to $1,000.

Business films. 10% of production cost on films up to $30,000. $150 per day. $20 per hour where % of cost not applicable.

Catalog ads/descriptions: $75 and up per page.

Comedy writing, for nightclub circuit entertainers. Gags only, $7 to $10. Routines, $100 to $300 a minute. Some new comics try to get 5-minute routines for $100 to $150, but top comics may pay $1,500 for a 5-minute bit from a top writer with credits.

Commercial reports, for business, insurance companies, credit agencies, market research firms. $5 to $10 per report.

Company newsletters, "house organs." $60 per page.

Consultation fees. $75 to $150 per hour.

Conventions, public relations for. $500 to $5,000.

Correspondent, magazine, regional. $8 to $20 per hour, plus expenses.

Criticism, art, music, drama, local. Free tickets plus $10 to $20.

Editing, freelance book. $8 per hour and up.

Educational film strips. $1,200.

Educational films, writing. $200 for one reeler (11 minutes of film); $1,000 to $1,500 for 30 minutes.

Educational grant proposals, writing. $75 to $175 per day, plus expenses.

Family histories, writing. $500 and up.

Fiction rewriting. $150 for 10-page short story to $10,000 for complete novel rewrite, under special circumstances.

Folders, announcement writing. $25 to $350.

Gallup Poll interviewing. $7 per hour.

Genealogical research, local. $4 to $8 per hour.

Ghostwriting full-length books. Same rate as "As told to" books.

Government, local, public information officer. $12 per hour, to $125 per day.

House organs, writing and editing. $65 to $400, 2 to 8 pp.

Industrial and business brochures, consultation, research, and writing. $3,500.

Industrial films. $500 to $1,200 10-minute reel; 5 to 12%

of the production cost of films that run $750 to $1,000 per release minute.

Industrial promotion. $10 to $60 per hour.

Industrial slide films. 14% of gross production cost.

Journalism, high school teaching, part-time. % of regular teacher's salary. Not less than $12 per hour.

Library, public relations. $5 to $25 per hour.

Magazine stringing, rates recommended by American Society of Journalists and Authors, Inc. 20¢ to $1 per word, based on circulation. Daily rate: $200 plus expenses. Weekly rate: $750 plus expenses.

New product releases or news releases. $200 and up.

Paperback cover copy. $50 and up.

Pharmacy newsletters. $125 to $300.

Photo-brochures. $700 to $15,000.

Political campaign writing. $300 to $500 per week; $35 per page piecework jobs.

Programmed instruction materials, writing $1,000 to $3,000 per hour of programmed training provided. Consulting/editorial fees: $25 per hour; $200 per day, plus expenses, minimum.

Public relations. $150 to $200 per day plus expenses.

Publicity writing. $40 per hour; $150 per day.

Radio copywriting. $75 and up per spot.

Record album cover copy. $200 to $400.

Retail business or financial business newsletters. $250 for 4 pages. $400 for 8 pages.

Retainer for fund-raising writing for a foundation. $500 to $750 per month.

Retainer for publicity and PR work for an adoption agency: $200 per month.

Retainer for writing for business, campaign funds. Usually a flat fee, but the equivalent of $10 to $20 per hour.

Reviews, art, drama, music, for national magazines. $25 to $50; $10 to $20 per column for newspapers.

School public relations. $4 to $12 per hour.

Shopping mall promotion. 15% of promotion budget for the mall.

Slide film, single image photo. $75.

Slide presentation for an educational institution. $1,000.

Speeches by writers who become specialists in certain fields. $200 to $2,000 plus expenses.

Sports information director, college. $1,000 to $2,500 per month. Professional: $2,000 to $4,000 per month.

Syndicated newspaper column, self-promoted. $7.50 weeklies; $6 to $50 per week for dailys, based on circulation.

Teaching creative writing, part-time. $15 to $50 per hour of instruction.

Teaching high school journalism, part-time. % of regular teacher's salary. Not less than $12 per hour.

Teaching home-bound students. $10 to $15 per hour.

Technical typing. 75¢ to $1.50 per page.

Technical typing masters for reproduction. $5 per hour for rough setup then $3 to $5 per page or $7 to $8 per hour.

Technical writing. $10 to $20 per hour.

Textbook and Tradebook copy editing. $5 to $8 per hour, or $1.00 per page.

Translation, literary. $25 to $50 per thousand words minimum.

Travel folder. $100 and up.

TV filmed news and features. $15 per film clip.

TV news film still photo. $5 to $20.

TV news story. $50 to $100.

This list gives you a general idea what to charge for your valuable writing services. Now let your own good judgment and availability make the final decision on "What's it Worth?"

METHODS OF BOOK PUBLISHING

There are three primary methods in which an author's book may be published. They are:

1. Accepted by a standard publishing house for publication.

2. Published by a "co-op" or "Vanity" type publisher.

3. Self-published by the author or by an independent publisher with the author's permission.

185

CONVENTIONAL LEGITIMATE PUBLISHERS

If a regular, reputable publishing company accepts your manuscript, they will pay all printing, production and promotional costs of turning your manuscript into a book.

Your success will solely depend on your book's merits and their promotion and distribution efforts. With the possible exception of a prearranged "advance" payment (difficult for unknown writers to obtain) any money you earn will come by way of a percentage of sales—known in the book trade as "royalties." Royalties range from 4% to 10% or even more. Today's average is around 6% to 8%. If your book sells well you can earn a nice profit; if it doesn't sell well, your profits will be very small. In either case, be it a smash hit or a real flop, you will not lose money on the printing, distribution, etc., since your publisher will pay all these expenses. You can only lose the time and effort it took you to write your book. Depending on how you value your time and efforts, this, too, can be a substantial loss if your book does not sell well. However, you will not be required to come up with "up-front publishing money."

VANITY PUBLISHERS, SUBSIDY PUBLISHERS, CO-OP PUBLISHERS AND DISTRIBUTORS, ETC.

Most Vanity-style publishers could care less about your book or booklet. They are, however, another means to "break into print." This is not a publishing method that is recommended by Russ von Hoelscher.

The game here, and it is a big money game, is to bring in the sheep and quickly fleece them. By using all sorts of hard-sell tactics and super-psychology concepts, vanity-type publishers (they also often hang out under subsidy and co-op publishing labels) do a huge, multimillion dollar business each year.

186

With few exceptions, I find "vanity" and "subsidy" publishers to be nothing more than literary con artists.

Regardless of the names they call themselves, the results are usually the same. The "publisher" implies that he will share the expenses with the author. He almost always is "thrilled" after reading the author's manuscript and strongly suggests the author sign his contract and "get published" at once. Usually, he states that many copies can be sold so that the author can not only get back his original investment, but also earn a "huge profit." Come on, baby, *we is going to make your book a best-seller. Sure they will!*

In recent years competition has become so fierce between these operators that their sophisticated sales literature began making more and more irrational statements, all promising authors great rewards for signing on the dotted line. So many complaints were filed with various government agencies that the Federal Trade Commission (FTC) finally was forced into action. They issued "cease and desist" orders against many Vanity and Co-op publishing companies. Many of those still in business have suits filed against them, but still continue to operate while fighting legal battles.

Before signing with any "publisher" (regardless of what name they use) who wants you to pay all publishing expenses in exchange for "future royalties," please write one or all of the below listed agencies:

Federal Trade Commission
Washington, D.C. 20540
(Ask them for a copy of all "complaints and decision" against Vanity-type publishers—then prepare for many hours of reading!)

Better Business Bureau of New York City
220 Church St.
New York, NY 10013
(Ask them for a report on "Vanity" publishers and also a reprint copy of "How to Get Published—More or Less"

187

which originally appeared in Harper's magazine.)

Many books, booklets and articles have exposed the sordid dealings of "Vanity" type publishers, telling how gullible authors have been ripped off. One of the best appeared in Lyle Stuart's *The Independent.* Send 50¢ and a self-addressed stamped envelope for a reprint of the eye-opening report on one man's experiences with a "subsidy" house to: The Independent, 239 Park Ave., South, New York, NY 10013.

For many years that I have been active as a writer, copywriter, self-publishing advisor and mail order consultant, I have talked with many, many authors who went through the Vanity publishing experience. Every person, with one exception, has told me they had a bad experience with a subsidy publisher. All had lost money and felt as if they had been taken. The lone defender of a Vanity publishing experience is a nice little lady in San Diego who had her collection of poems published at a cost of almost five grand with a vanity house. She freely admits less than 100 copies were sold and that she lost almost all of her investment. Still, she is happy.

"I wanted my poems in book format without doing any of the production work myself. This they did for me, and I'm pleased."

If she is happy, I'm happy for her. And if you are interested in "seeing" your work in print and are willing to cough up five thousand smackers or more for the privilege, you have a right to do it. However, I'm sure most of my readers will agree with me when I say: I can't afford to mess around with these city slickers. Me thinks an author's money interests subsidy houses a zillion times more than the author's words that are put to paper.

SELF-PUBLISHING

The third and often best method that can be used to get

188

your book or booklet into print is the do-it-yourself publish and promote it method!

Using this concept you pay the full printing costs, but you also get all copies printed. You deal with a book printer whose only job is to print and ship you your books as soon as possible. You become the publisher, promoter and prime source. You alone take responsibility for your book, booklet, report, etc., and the ultimate success or failure.

Self-publishing is not new. Among the great authors of all time are many who at one time or other turned to do-it-yourself publishing including Shelley, Mark Twain, Walt Whitman, Upton Sinclair, William Blake and Zane Grey.

In more modern times Carl Sandburg, D.H. Lawrence, and James Joyce have joined the ranks of the self-published. Conventional publishers told Lawrence his book, *Lady Chatterly's Lover*, was pornographic; James Joyce's *Ulysses* was just too long; Sandburg has a history of adverse relations with standard publishers and Bob Ringer's *Winning Through Intimidation* was rejected so many times he decided to go it alone. Single-handedly he made it a big financial success and then sold reprint rights for a fortune to the same type of conventional publisher who previously had only passed out a pink slip.

Recently, hundreds of self-publishers have been making their mark and their fortune by publishing their own works. This list includes Robert Ringer, Dr. Wayne Dyer, Mark O. Haroldsen, Joe Karbo and Howard Ruff. Although there are success stories in many different fields, business and finance has launched more smashing best-sellers than any other.

IS SELF-PUBLISHING FOR YOU?

Too many writers remain obscure and broke because they live in the secluded, unrealistic world of the "artist." If you look down your nose at the business end of writing and find something crass about promotion advertising and making a profit, self-publishing is not for you! Chances are, you'll never make much money from your literary labors, regardless of how you market them. To make money you need a positive attitude about money. If you see yourself as a struggling author who disdains commercial success, rest easy. Success will not invade your private domain.

If, however, you get excited about the do-it-yourself approach to writing and publishing, and even more pumped-up about earning a small or large fortune, self-publishing could be your road to riches.

Professionals (doctors, ministers, lawyers, college professors, etc.) often turn to self-publishing as a means to an end. Since greater recognition and prestige follow authorship, they often self-publish to build or maintain a professional image. While their book may not be a smashing commercial success, as an author they are elevated to the extreme in the eyes of friends, relatives and their peer group.

A recent national poll showed how highly authors were respected in America. Among the "Most Admired Professions" writers ranked fourth highest. Only rock singers, movie stars and sports heroes ranked higher.

An author will be elevated to extremes in the eyes of friends, relatives and his peer group, regardless of whether his book is successful or not. Doctors, psychologists, lawyers, teachers, ministers and other professionals often gain greater status by writing and publishing a book in a specialized field. A book written on a specialized topic often tends to make others believe the author is an "expert" in that certain area. Often this promotes increased opportunities, a better position, a large salary increase, public speaking or consulting fees, etc.

It's a fact! A large number of people secretly would like to write a book. An even larger segment of the population is impressed by those who do.

190

PUBLISHING FOR PROFITS

I certainly have nothing against folks who become authors because of the fame and prestige associated with publishing their own books. I accept this as a legitimate reason to go into print. After all, even if their books do not earn them a nice profit, better positions and increased earning potentials are often a byproduct of self-publishing. Thus, in the long run, their books or reports may pave the way for future substantial earnings.

Prestige and recognition is a worthwhile reason to self-publish. However, I do have a special fondness for the self-publishing author who "publishes for profits."

Making money is the name of the game! It's fun, too! This author has written more than three dozen books and manuals on various subjects: writing, publishing, mail order, direct mail, advertising, real estate, professional football, horse racing, etc. Add to this hundreds of published articles and fillers, and also newsletter and magazine publishing. Not to mention my main area of expertise—copywriting!—countless ads, circulars, catalogs, sales letters, et al. I love it, and recommend it to all self-starters!

The big money is here for the positive thinking, positive action self-publisher. Next to a burning desire to succeed and a good measure of knowledge and self-confidence, success is usually the result of one's willingness to get involved and master the business of promotion, sales, advertising and distribution. Writing your book or booklet is only step one on the long ladder that can lead to a smashing success in self-publishing. An author could write one of the greatest books ever, but if he stops there, his self-publishing venture will fail. Effective promotion and marketing are the major self-publishing success factors. A good idea for a book, newsletter, etc., is not good enough. Who will pay for it? How do you reach them? What is your marketing strategy? The answer to these, and other promotion and marketing questions, is essential to your success. The wrong answers (or not asking the questions in the first place) brings failure.

191

SUCCESSFUL BOOK DISTRIBUTION

Writing a book is only a job 10% to 20% complete. There is joy in seeing your literary labors "born" through the printing process. If you have decided to let a legitimate publishing company (not a flim-flam subsidy outfit, I hope, for your sake) publish your masterpiece and they have accepted, 80% of the work (marketing and sales) lies ahead, but your effort is completed. If you're going to self-publish, you had better get to work! A lack of sales, promotion and distribution effort can turn even a good book into a financial dud.

You gotta *tell 'em to sell 'em*, and that means hustle and bustle in the arena of sales and publicity.

While it's not that difficult now for writers to self-publish their own works, the novice publisher will soon discover publication is only the first step on the ladder of success in self-publishing. It is the vital areas of distribution and marketing that will decide ultimate victory or defeat of any publishing venture.

Too often writers/publishers order 1,000 or more books, manuals or booklets printed, and then ask themselves, "How am I going to get them distributed and sold?"

Friends and relatives are only going to put a very small dent in a 1,000 book run, unless the author is immensely popular and has a huge circle of friends or fans. Successful distribution strategy begins prior to publication, not as an afterthought while staring at many boxes of your books stacked high in your garage or spare bedroom.

Here are just some of the proven ways to sell books, (many of them very innovative):

- Sell through a book distributor
- Sell direct to bookstores
- Sell to libraries and schools

- Sell via telephone solicitation
- Sell via mail order space ads
- Sell via direct mail
- Sell through radio and TV commercials
- Sell at swap meets and flea markets
- Sell door to door
- Sell at local parks and recreation areas
- Sell by handing out ad flyers at concerts, churches, conventions, universities, etc.

Every one of the abovementioned techniques of selling self-published books has been used successfully to market the written word. At first glance, a few of these methods may seem very unusual, but they have worked for others—why not for you? If you abhor lots of personal contact with potential book buyers, some of the above distribution techniques will not be your cup of tea. You'll have to try more conventional sales tactics (working with distributors, retailers, etc.); however, if you don't mind "getting involved" with people to sell your books, your means of distribution can cover the gamut of distribution methods. Many, if not all, of the above, plus many more you can experiment with.

The real secret of successful book distribution is to EXPAND YOUR THINKING. "Think sales!"

Get busy telling people about the merits of your book. "THE MORE YOU TELL, THE MORE YOU SELL." Remember William H. Johnsen's ten important two-letter words: "IF IT IS TO BE, IT IS UP TO ME!"

HOW TO SELL BOOKSTORES

If you self-publish, you must market. You don't market to stores or institutions, you market to people. Here are some of the proven methods of *how to sell bookstores* (the women and men who operate them, of course) your book. I am discussing a full-size book or manual. Small folios, reports, etc., may be excellent sellers via mail order, with folks eager to pay good money for the information provided. However, when it comes to selling your wares on bookshop shelves, your offering better look a lot like the competition—a book that looks like a book!

Once a bookstore owner or manager has agreed to handle your book, you have given it a competitive chance. It will either sell or not sell based on its own merits, or at least, based on bookshop customers' willingness to part with cash money for what you have written. True, further promotion and advertising, plus selective display can greatly enhance its saleability. Still, just being allowed "space" on the shelves gives it at least a fighting chance in the open literary marketplace.

Self-published books, booklets and manuals are receiving more attention today than any time previously. They have now become *almost acceptable* in the book selling community. Some booksellers are still resisting the new wave of self-published books. While their reasoning is many-fold, a few "reasons" store owners offer are:

- Dealing with a book distributor makes bookkeeping easier
- Previous bad experiences with a self-publisher or "slow selling" self-published work
- Limited shelf space
- Book and/or author lacks recognition

SOME SOLUTIONS

The book dealer who objects to "billing" from many different sources should be told something similar to this: "Let's forget about billing. I'll give you an extra 5% discount for cash" (of course, you'll take a check!), *or* "Let's put 5 or 10 copies of my book here on consignment

—you only pay after they sell, and if they don't sell, it hasn't cost you anything."

Both of the above techniques may break down initial resistance. You may win the dealer over in your flexibility and desire to do business on his terms. But be reasonable. Don't move into their bookstore. Maybe this guy (or gal) has had to contend with a "pushy" self-published author previously. Do get your book placed on the best display shelves available for maximum exposure. Don't drop in two or three times a day to "check on how sales are going." Once a week is about right, unless you have a good rapport with the dealer and he enjoys talking "shop" with you. If it's strictly a business arrangement and you perceive you are dealing with a coolly efficient type—play the game to the hilt. Let him know in advance that he won't see you again for at least "a week or more." This should put his mind to rest that he is not dealing with "a flaky, eager-beaver, bothersome writer!"

Lack of space is a hard objection to overcome, but where there's a will, there's just got to be a way! A friend of mine who operates a small book distributing company in the San Diego area showed me one great way to overcome the "limited space" syndrome for books he wanted placed at a certain downtown bookshop. The solution? Take off your sports jacket (if you're wearing one), roll up your sleeves— and get busy! Busy showing the bookshop owner or manager alternative display methods. Be careful not to give him the impression that he is not a good displayer. Simply, make a few calculated suggestions that can benefit him—and you! Using this approach, my distributor friend "found" shelf space for 50 titles he was distributing—surely you can find room for a few copies of your book!

Regarding the quality (the printing) of your book: If it is not a decent, attractive quality job, you're in trouble. The major publishers crank out high quality workmanship. To compete, you better make sure your book printer can produce a competitive product. Many self-publishers who deal exclusively in mail order sales may specialize in low quality books. After all, they often reason, "It's the ad that sells the book." This is not the case when your book is sitting on the bookstore shelf surrounded by thousands of other titles. Yes, the subject matter is very important but "looks" count big too. Very few poor-quality books sell at retail outlets. A well printed book with an attractive cover is a must! Also, don't neglect the back cover. Once a prospective customer has picked up some of the book's major benefits (reasons to purchase) can close the sale. More often than not, the front cover and the title get the attention, but it's the back cover copy that makes the sale! If you leave the back cover blank or indulge in only a little self-appeasing, glory-seeking with much to do "about the author," you can miss closing the sale.

The above problems and some possible solutions all concern themselves with "face to face" direct selling. Now let's turn our attention to profitable ways to solicit book dealers by mail.

You forfeit an important selling tool—"eyeball to eyeball salesmanship" when you solicit booksellers by mail. Now it is vital that you employ a nice printed circular and/or sales letter to make your presentation pay off.

Since retail bookstores are constantly being bombarded by book publishers and wholesalers, you will want to use every sales technique possible to get your message across and an order placed.

A nice topical book, well printed with an attractive cover, is a must! If the cover of your book is a real knockout, I recommend having your printer make a photocopy—approximately 2"x3" and print it on your sales letter and/or circular.

Now what other sales inducement can you offer each prospective bookseller? What about your discount?

A 40% discount off cover price is the normal discount in the book trade. The big chain stores often get another 5%, but 40% off cover is pretty standard.

A 50% DISCOUNT COULD
SWING THE SALE!

If you can afford to offer a 50% discount (or more!) on your book (and most self-publishers can!), by all means do it! This type of premium discount gets welcomed attention from many book dealers.

The extra 10% off will not get an order from the dealer who sees no other value in handling your book, but if he is seriously considering ordering, the extra discount could well "sell him" on placing the order. It can be the deciding factor!

I have had success with many of my self-published works in offering a full 50% discount, combined with a request for payment with order. I consider this a very productive trade-off. I give the dealer an extra 10% discount that he appreciates, and I get paid with receipt of the order, something I really consider a coup!

Since many booksellers are notoriously slow in paying their bills (some *never* pay them!), a check with order can eliminate a future hassle. Keep in mind, terms of payment with order will only be honored by the one-location dealers. Large chains of bookstores, drugstores, discount outlets, etc., insist on 30-day billing. Don't let this stop you. Large chains overall have a good record of paying their bills promptly. Individual bookshops comprise about 80% of all stores in the USA and Canada, but don't overlook the other 20% controlled by large chains.

This circular brought home the bacon! I had a good book tailormade for California retailers. I offered an attractive full 50% off discount and mailed to the right list. I purchased a mailing list of 350 newsstands that sold the California edition of the Racing Form. In addition, my girl Friday spent one day at the local library and compiled a list of bookshops from various phone directories: Los Angeles, San Diego, San Francisco, Sacramento, San Jose, and other leading statewide cities and towns. A mailing to 1,250 retailers resulted in more than 100 orders. Two weeks after the mailing, the best was yet to come as many dealers repeated with large reorders!

SELL YOURSELF—
THEN SELL THE BOOK DEALERS

A positive, assertive approach is essential if you intend to convince bookshop owners that they are well-advised to carry your books. This is true in both face-to-face selling or mail order solicitation. If you develop self-confidence in yourself and really objective "good feelings" about your book, your oral or written sales pitch is going to be that much more powerful. If your book has any merit whatsoever, the only obstruction in your path is any reluctance of book retailers to stock and display it. The correct oral or written presentation will win them over. This can spell S-U-C-C-E-S-S for your book!!

SELLING LIBRARIES

Although librarians have traditionally been a good friend to self-publishers and small presses, severe budget cuts have restricted their buying power. Where once they could order 5 copies of a new book, they often only order a single copy, unless they are convinced the book will be in high demand. I recommend today's self-publisher restrict his or her library market to the larger institutions—those libraries who have a book buying budget of $25,000 or more, annually. You can either secure a library distributor to handle this market for you, or promote by mail during the early spring or fall months, which is the library season for new book procurement.

Librarians are greatly influenced by favorable reviews. A

good review in a major library trade journal, will definitely help you sell your book.

SELLING WORDS TO
THE BIG CATALOG HOUSES

America's leading mail order catalog houses (Spencer Gifts, Sunset House, Hanover House, etc.) reach tens of millions of active mail order buyers yearly. These mass media catalog mailers specialize in mailing attractive gift and novelty catalogs 4 to 8 times per year. Each catalog is crammed with hundreds of items geared for impulse mail order buying. Additionally, most of the major catalog mailers also run "leader" space ads in popular magazines: *House Beautiful, Apartment Living,* etc., to generate new customers. While the majority of the items they carry fall into the gift, toy and novelty merchandise classification, they also sell millions of dollars worth of books, booklets and folios yearly. Recently I have noted these subjects were being offered: *Handwriting Analysis, Astrology, Winning Contests, Tracing Your Family Roots, Numerology, Writing and Self-Publishing, Playing Poker* and *Playing Bingo.* You can see, this represents a wide spectrum of subjects. No doubt, many other subjects are also being peddled or would be found acceptable for mass marketing by this often overlooked, but big-dollar market.

BIG DISCOUNTS FOR BIG SHIPMENTS

A few years ago, *Mr. Bingo,* Gus Levy, sold 40,000 36-page booklets to a dozen different leading catalog houses. He earned very attractive profits, even though his profit-per-book was very modest. You can't earn a whole lot per book when you're selling your wares at 40¢ per copy as Gus did. However, even 10¢ net profit per book (and Gus probably earned much more) ain't all that bad when you do it 40,000 times. Gus says he made out okay. In case you were wondering, the catalog firms sold his bingo book in the low retail price range of 99¢ to $2, with the "average" retail price being $1.50. Far less than the $3 per copy Gus received from his own advertising.

If you have the right book or folio for this wide-open market, you're going to have to bait your sales hook with a bigger than normal discount. The big catalog merchandise buyers turn their noses up at standard 40% and 50% book discounts. Nothing less than 60% is likely to be considered, and it may take discounts of 70% or more to really grab their attention.

If you enjoy low cost per unit publishing and if you have a stimulating, informational self-help or how-to-do-it title, this broad market could be tailormade for you.

Standard soliciting procedure is to send a sample copy of your book, any available advertising material and a personalized letter spelling out your offer and your best wholesale prices. Three prices should be sufficient: per 100, 500 and 1,000 units ordered.

Four of the biggest catalog houses are listed below (check out a recent issue of *House Beautiful* or other "homes type" magazine for other current advertisers.

SUNSET GIFTS
12800 Culver Blvd., Los Angeles, CA 90066

SPENCER GIFTS
1050 Black Horse Pike, Atlantic City, NJ 08410

HANOVER HOUSE
Hanover, PA 17331

FOSTER-TRENT
2345 Boston Post Rd., Larchmont, NY 10538

PUBLISHING A NEWSLETTER

Kiplinger is given credit for launching the newsletter concept 20 years ago, and by the mid 1970s the tremendous newsletter explosion was in full swing. The 1980s were the biggest and best decade ever for informative newsletters, especially financial letters, and this trend is expected to continue into the 1990s.

There seems to be a need for newsletter publishing under every possible subject heading. Folks today desire specialized information on a thousand and one different topics. From *religion* to *astrology* and from the *stock market advice* to *blackjack systems,* successful newsletters set the pace in providing fast-breaking news, inside info, tips and predictions.

SELL YOUR KNOWLEDGE— DON'T KEEP IT TO YOURSELF OR GIVE IT AWAY

Leading newsletter publishers like Howard Ruff of the *Ruff Times,* are cashing in big on selective knowledge. *The Ruff Times* currently has over 150,000 subscribers at about $95 per one-year subscription. That puts yearly N/L revenue in the neighborhood of fifteen million dollars. A darn nice neighborhood to reside in. Sure, Howard Ruff is the exception, not the rule. Nevertheless, hundreds of other newsletter publishers are making nice profits. So can you if you have the right idea, good information, and above all else, a powerful marketing strategy.

YOUR SUBJECT SHOULD
RELATE TO YOUR INTERESTS

If you're serious about entering the newsletter field, do so with a subject that you excel in. Be it business opportunities, stocks, entertainment, product information, self-improvement, consumer advice, or what have you? Just make sure you have the specialized knowledge to start your letter and a keen interest that will push you deeper into your subject and related areas. It will help if you are an avid reader. Usually one must read many books, magazines, newspapers, trade journals, etc., in order to cull new information of value to your subscribers. An elaborate filing system may be required to file interesting facts from your research.

FORMAT

The standard format of a newsletter is either one or two 11x17 sheets printed on both sides and folded to 8½x11 size.

A four-page letter is one 11x17 sheet and an eight-page letter is two such sheets. While most letters are either 4 or 8 pages, some publishers produce a 6-pager. This is easily done. One 11x17 sheet printed both sides and folded, plus an inserted 8½x11 sheet printed both sides and left unfolded, makes a six-page newsletter. While there is no rigid rule saying all newsletters must be 4 or 6 or 8 pages in the 8½x11 format, 95% do fall into this format.

OVERALL NEWSLETTER COST

While newsletter production costs are quite low (5,000 copies of an 8-page newsletter can be typeset and printed for around $1,000—about 20¢ each—and if typesetting is not required you can cut that cost substantially), subscription solicitation costs are very high. As 1988 begins, the average yearly subscription rate is approximately $90, according to a nationwide newsletter reporting poll. (The range greatly varies: from just a couple of dollars to a couple thousand dollars per yearly subscription.)

Newsletter publishers, even the top producers, often spend 100% of the subscription price for every new subscriber they bag! Thus a $100 per year letter may well spend $100 or more for *every new subscriber obtained*. How on earth can you make a profit if it takes 100% of all new subscription revenue just to procure new members, you ask? Your answer follows:

REPEAT PROFITS

While it is common in the industry to spend 80% to 120% or more of all new subscription money just to land those subscriptions, exciting financial gains are still available to the diligent publisher. The key to success here is in generating a *high renewal percentage*. It may have cost you an outlandish sum for every new member obtained, but you may only spend one dollar or less in receiving each renewal. Three or four months prior to a subscription expiring, the dedicated writer/publisher begins sending out renewal notices. The first "notice" is a very soft sell. You simply inform your subscriber that his/her subscription expires soon and ask them to renew now.

If two such general notices haven't brought your subscriber back into the flock, you or an expert advertising copywriter must produce the right appeal that will convince the subscriber that he absolutely must continue receiving your valuable letter, that it is *vital to him* that he receive it without interruption.

Since it is 98% less costly to have a current subscriber renew than to obtain a brand new one, you must keep sending renewal literature. No less than four attempts should be made to reinstate a subscriber.

A high renewal rate spells S-U-C-C-E-S-S in newsletter publishing. A good topical letter should bring a high renewal rate. Most experts agree that you must have at least 40% of your clients repeat if you are to win the war of attrition and establish a self-sustaining, money-making letter. The super pros shoot for a 60% or better renewal rate!

Starting a newsletter from scratch can call for a considerable investment, and profits will be slim or non-existent for the first 12-18 months in this business. Remember, profits come from renewals, seldom from first-time subscribers. Often it is better to self-publish a book, and use your book as a means to launch a newsletter to people with similar interests. It is so much more cost-effective to solicit newsletter subscribers from your own customer base, than to start a newsletter from scratch.

MORE LETTERS
FOR CASH

CREDIT AND COLLECTION
WRITING SERVICE

While several major corporations maintain their own in-house collection agency or do business with a large outside bill collection service, most business people do not.

Thousands of firms need a freelancer who can help develop new business and establish credit for them. Also much needed, is a sharp writing style to induce slow accounts to *pay up!*

Drumming up business: If you live in a city or good-sized town, personal contact (go up one side of the street and down the other) will land you clients. If you live away from a metropolitan area, or just prefer not to play salesman, direct mail can be used to build your business.

WHAT MAKES 'EM PAY? Simple! *Pride, guilt or fear!* Good collection letters incorporate a strong appeal to one of those three motives. You'll have to play psychologist when analyzing slow-pays. Individualized letters bring the best results. Your first letter should always be short and to the point, but also quite friendly. A simple "you no doubt have overlooked this bill..." request usually will suffice. From letter #2 to the **Final Notice** (usually not till 3 or 4 previous attempts have failed), your persuasive skills can make you lots of money.

Standard fee for collection: 40% of debt owed your client. If the debt is quite current (120 days or less) you might take a smaller percentage. Likewise, you ought to receive no less than 60% if the debt is "cold," over one year old. You should also inform your customers that they must consider discounting old debts. Example: another firm owes your client $500 but the debt is 14 months cold. After all else has proved unfruitful, you may wish to offer a "final notice and proposed settlement." If the wayward company or person will pay within 10 days, you will discount the debt 40%, thus accepting $300 as payment in full. This action often brings fast payment on an otherwise uncollectable account. Just make sure all of the discount money isn't subtracted from your fee. Your client must share the discount with you, the collection writer.

There is no standard fee for establishing new business or arranging credit. You will have to negotiate your own best deal. One good method is to determine approximate time involved, making darn sure you receive no less than $15 per hour for this important service.

OPERATE A HOBBY LETTER

If you are enthusiastic to the point of being full tilt bozo on a certain hobby, game or sport, consider a letter on the subject. Successful word profits are to be made in almost every aspect of human recreational activity.

FAMILY NAME LETTER PROFITS

Here's a dashing new concept with unlimited fun and money potential! Why not take advantage of the *trace your own roots* craze that has hit America and Canada ever since Alex Haley wrote his ten-million copy bestseller *Roots* a few years ago.

If you're interested in your own family tree and if you don't hate research, this is a natural! You begin by tracing

206

your family name as far back as you can. You then solicit subscribers from folks with your name (city telephone books usually are the worst source of names for a direct mail campaign, but not so using this exciting plan—they give you a source of free names and addresses to mail to!). Since a person's name is like beautiful music to his or her ears, a family name newsletter is a potential source of huge revenue. Once you get beyond the historical aspects of your name, get full participation from your subscribers. Request that they send in a profile on themselves. Also you can print as many addresses in each issue as space permits, encouraging members to get to know each other better.

Regarding subscription rates: methinks a social newsletter like this is, demands a rather reasonable subscription fee. Perhaps $15 to $20 per year for a monthly letter (12 times yearly) or $8 to $10 for a bimonthly (6 times per annum would be about right).

A hobby letter and family-name letter may be started from scratch on a limited budget, but it may take awhile (several months) to realize a profit.

RESUME PROFITS

In today's competitive job market, well-prepared resumes are increasingly vital in landing the better jobs. Resumes are designed to give employers a brief, but penetrating look at the background and qualifications of prospective employees. The busy employer saves time, effort and money by qualifying job applicants through the resume process.

The need for well-prepared resumes has created a multimillion dollar market for word sellers. The money is good and the work relatively easy when you *follow the wheel* (the established format).

Some writers found resume writing so very profitable that they have turned to it exclusively, often setting up storefront shops in busy downtown areas. Other word sellers use resume writing as just part and parcel of their total sales approach to writing for pay.

RESUME WRITING FACTORS

The main object of the resume is to get your job seekers hired. Great for word-of-mouth advertising! To accomplish this task you must embellish their positive past employment history and any and all other pleasing work and personal traits. Among key points an employer wants to see in a resume are:

208

1. APPLICANT'S OBJECTIVE—The exact position the applicant is applying for and his/her major qualifications for same.

2. EMPLOYMENT HISTORY—List positions previously held with description of all services rendered. A full description of a person's last held job is required. Prior to this, the skillful resume writer may be somewhat selective in listing past employment. For example, it may be prudent not to mention a position in the past where the applicant was discharged or forced to quit under undesirable circumstances.

3. EDUCATION—Here we list data on our job-seeker's highest education achievements. List name of the college or high school and subjects majored in and any degrees that were earned. Also, list any on-the-job education the applicant pursued outside of his formal education.

4. PERSONALIZED INFORMATION—Although optional, it is often well advised to list the civic, social and charitable organizations a person is affiliated with. Caution: if your client is a political or social activist, with membership in some highly volatile organization, it may be best to omit this information, unless of course, you know the person who is in charge of hiring shares a similar viewpoint.

The standard resume is only one or two pages in length. However, size and content vary greatly. Ten pages may be appropriate for the person seeking a "big job." The fee a word seller can charge for resumes also varies. On the average $7 to $12 for a simple "short form" resume of one or two pages would seem about right. Add at least $4 or $5 for every additional page over two. Often your clients will request several copies of the same resume you prepare. They should be run off on a good copier. If you don't own a quality desk model plain bond copier, make arrangements with a local printer who has one. Your client should not only pay the actual cost of making copies, but also a couple extra dollars for your effort. Example: You charge your client $10 for a two-page resume and $1 for each additional copy.

SOLICITING RESUME CLIENTS

As mentioned, some resume writers have opened resume stores in busy areas of cities, enjoying walk-in trade. Short of this, small ads in leading local newspapers, tabloids and magazines will usually attract eager customers. College papers and bulletins also produce clients.

Sample ad copy:

RESUMES. Get that special job.
Have your resume professionally
prepared. Low cost! Call 000-0000.

Supplies needed are minimal: A ream of white bond paper, carbon paper, correcting fluid and your trusty typewriter will get you started. Also, if you don't own a copying machine, you must at least have the use of one nearby.

Following is a hypothetical resume to give you further insight into format:

RESUME

James Hill
1202 Mission Street
San Diego, CA 90000
Phone: (619) 000-0000

OBJECTIVE

TO OBTAIN A POSITION WHICH OFFERS ME A CHALLENGE AND OPPORTUNITY FOR ADVANCEMENT.

EMPLOYMENT

FOOD TOWN MARKET   5/81 to 6/83
610 Main Street, San Diego, CA   Position: produce manager

As produce manager for the large (over 17,000 square feet) Food Town Market in San Diego, my responsibilities included supervision of the 2,000 square foot "produce department", including selections and purchase of all fruits and vegetables. During the two years I worked for Food Town, produce business increased 20%.

JACK'S FOOD MART   4/80 to 5/81
100 Pacifica Avenue, San Diego, CA

I worked in many different capacities while at Jack's Food Mart. I served as check-out clerk, stock man, meat counter assistant and produce worker. Also, I drove the company truck and accompanied owner, Jack Swanson, on meat and produce market buying trips.

DISCOUNT DRUGS   2/78 to 4/80
777 Seacliff Street, San Diego, CA

Worked part-time for Discount Drugs while attending business college. Approximately 25 hours weekly. While most of my duties were confined to the stock room, I also worked as a clerk in both the cosmetic and candy departments.

EDUCATION
6/78 to 6/80   SEASIDE BUSINESS COLLEGE
                                                          San Diego, CA
                                          MAJOR: Business Economics
                                                  Complete 2 year course

PERSONAL DATA
Height: 6'1"
Weight: 185 lbs.
Health: Excellent
Marital status: Married on March 16, 1983
Organizations: PTA, Helping Hands Association
Interests: Swimming, waterskiing, guitar, spectator sports

211

SHOPPER PROFITS

Maggie McCoy Turnbull owns and operates the *New England Express Shopper* that serves three small Massachusetts coastal towns. Her weekly tabloid began as only a four-pager, and with only six paid advertisers. By issue #3 she doubled the size (8 pages) and could boast thirty-nine display advertisers plus over 100 classified ads. By issue #5, again she enjoyed double the pages (now 16) plus 60 display advertisers and more than 200 classified ads. More importantly, within five short weeks she was making a profit. Not bad for a small, three-person tabloid (two teenage daughters help her play publisher, editor, writer, advertising salesperson, business manager, distributor (all copies are free), janitor and bookkeeper. Not bad at all when you consider she started her shopper with just slightly over two thousand dollars.

Maggie's big secret? *"I worked 60 hours a week, mostly calling on local merchants for advertising. Most were afraid to go with an unproven new paper, even though my ad rates were very cheap. However, enough said okay that my shopper began to grow rapidly."* I hope many!

Most shoppers, like Maggie's, are tabloids, printed offset on the big web-fed presses. Standard format: 5 columns in width by 16 inches in depth. Approximately 80 column inches per page. The tabloid page size is much larger than a magazine, but smaller than most daily papers. An eight-page shopper with five 16-inch columns per page will yield about 500 inches of ad space. Now let's say you kick off your weekly with a 5,000 circulation (it is risky to start any paper with less than a 5,000 run). Here is an example of weekly costs and potential profits.

5,000 8-page tabloids (newsprint) typeset, printed and folded: $500.

Distribution (the paper itself is FREE!) costs to deliver to homes and businesses: $125.

Overhead—office machinery and supplies, office rent, utilities, phone, etc. (per week): $125.

TOTAL: $775 each week.

POTENTIAL PROFITS

60 display advertisers, averaging 5 inches of space each—300 inches @ $6 per col. inch: $1,800.

200 classified (business and personal) advertisers @ $1 per ad (shopper publishers have found it is good biz to practically give away classifieds—some actually do give them away FREE—to get several people in the habit of using the paper): $200.

Okay, it is only hypothetical! Yet lots of people are making it work. If you spend $775 a week to do business and you take in $2,000, your weekly profit is very attrative. Most shopper publishers settle for a lot less, especially during the critical first few months. Our example did not include extra advertising salespeople that many shoppers employ on a strictly commission basis. In our figures, we assumed the publisher was bringing in all the ad business. If you sign up another salesperson or two, you'll have to allow them at least 20% of revenue from each ad they sell. And in order to keep a good *ad hustler,* many publishers offer up to 40% of money from ads they sell. This can cut into profits. Also, shopper publishers often have to "open accounts" for local business people. Some of these independent merchants go

213

under without paying off their advertising account, others stay in biz and still refuse to pay, often claiming "no results."

RESULTS BUILD REPEAT BUSINESS

You have seen the profit potential on just 8 pages. Increase to 12, 16, 20 or more and the numbers soar! Even with more payouts and a few no-pays, the publisher can make the big bucks. Here are some major factors that bring success.

(1) You find a need (little or no nearby competition from another strong shopper or powerful daily). Anyone considering starting a shopper should spend as much time as possible "talking shop" with local merchants. Especially seek their reaction regarding their local advertising or lack of same.

(2) If you go for it, do it right—*publish an attractive paper*. Pay heed to overall design and select a "catchy" name or one that fits your locale.

(3) Pound the pavement. *Seek out your advertisers. Once you're well established (in business over one year) and if your reputation as a customer producer is good, they will begin to seek you. Until then you must keep after them. The big chain supermarkets, drug, discount, and variety stores probably will ignore you until they have noticed you have a well-established paper. So, your main ad meat will be the small independent stores and shops of all varieties. Don't be too selective, go up and down the street.*

(4) *Make sure the paper gets distributed.* Foolish indeed is the novice shopper owner who does a good job in getting a steady flow of ad dollars only to get sloppy in regard to distribution. No! You don't hire a couple of high school kids, pay them a measly amount and forget about it! Two reliable high schoolers may be great as your distribution crew, but if you're wise, you'll monitor their services. Even if your own son or daughter is one of your helpers, keep tabs

214

on distribution. Repeat advertising is essential to a shopper's success. Repeat ad dollars only come from happy merchants who have received results! Good distribution brings buyers and sellers together.

(5) 120 Days To Success! *Stick with it if it shows any sign of possible success.* Most shoppers that do fold (well over half do) go under within the first four months. Some go down in less than four weeks! Hang in there. After 3 or 4 months, the odds switch over to your side. It is the old *winners never quit and quitters never win* syndrome that nevertheless is so true in many areas of business, writing, publishing—and life!

MORE POINTERS THAT LEAD TO PROFITS

- Seek out a reliable web printer for your tabloid. (Ditto for typesetting and composition.)

- Time the initial issue late in the month so that you can quickly bill your advertisers on the first of the following (this is a good trick to play if cash flow is vital from the start).

- Although advertising pays the bills and makes the profit, "save" at least 20% of each issue for human interest news reporting.

- A big tip! People love their names in print. Make an effort to list as many people in each issue as possible. Keep tabs on all local events—women's clubs, girl scouts, boy scouts, high school sports and activities, etc. At first you'll have to seek out newsy items. As soon as local folks realize you seek such items, they will bring them to you.

- Regular columns on local gossip, recipes, even astrology, can build reader interest. Yes, you may have to pay for this. You just can't be the cook, the chief gossip, the den mother and the star gazer too! Give local writers a chance. $20 to $40 is the going rate for a column (300 to 800 words) in a small local paper. Perhaps you can trade some leftover ad space for the words you need.

You can prosper with a Shopper. Many factors add up to success or failure. Next to a burning determination to own and operate your own successful paper, location is the key. Following location is area to cover (it must be well defined) and then comes competition. If you discover an area with little or no competition or unimaginative competition, you have found a need. Fill it!

SELL INFORMATION

Publishing full-sized books is not the only way to make a lucrative living as a writer/self-publisher. Thousands of women and men are making excellent profits selling simple, but important information by mail. Everything from mouth-watering recipes to trade source directories to how to repair a Volkswagen can be, and is being marketed.

A case in point: last summer I decided to get away from my work for a while. Since I had an open invitation from Avery and Denny Treon to visit them and Denny's family in Veneta, Oregon, just outside of Eugene, I decided this was the perfect retreat for me. The scenery in this part of the country is beautiful, just as it is here in Southern California, but there are a whole lot less people in Oregon. Sometimes that's nice. Kick back and relax with friends. That we did. No talk of publishing, promoting and advertising. That did not happen!

My friend Denny, a gifted guitar player who has played rock, folk and country all over the nation (he once was with Dick Dale's band—Dick is the famous surf-guitar originator). Now that he is married to a wonderful lady named Kate, and has four lovely kids, he has settled down. No more road shows or all-night gigs. What now for my friend? He's selling information by mail. Denny has perfected a revolutionary new lead-guitar system. He calls it *The Method**. He sells it by mail!

I did unwind up in Oregon. We drank a few brews and

swapped a few tales. I even persuaded Denny to sing some of Bob Dylan's early songs, which I love, and which he does so well. But if I thought there was going to be no mail order, publishing and marketing talk, *God didn't make little green apples and it don't rain in Minneapolis—or Oregon.*

Denny wanted to know everything about my writing, publishing and marketing activities, and I wanted to know about his unique information system.

I love my chosen profession. How could I ever go a full week without "shop talk?" It can't happen!

If you have some good information in your head, or are willing to do some research to get it, put it down on paper. Print it and/or record it and sell it by mail. Rich rewards are available.

Another man from the Pacific Northwest whom I respect and like, discovered a secret way to rid his farm of moles and gophers. He typed up his valuable secret on two pieces of paper, printed and sold it through small classified ads. Today, he is well known and respected as an author, and the publisher of *Towers Club-USA* **. His name is Jerry Buchanan, and his information selling advice has helped thousands of men and women achieve success (including million dollar success!) in information by mail marketing.

Like I said, *Rich Rewards* are available to today's sharp information by mail marketers.

_____

*If you're into music and are interested in my friend's quick-learn lead guitar system, write for more information to: THE METHOD, P.O. Box 954, Veneta, OR 97487.

**If you would like more information on Jerry Buchanan's "Towers Club-USA" newsletter for writers, publishers and information by mail sellers, write: Towers Club-USA, P.O. Box 2038, Vancouver, WA 98661.

SPEAK OUT
FOR PROFITS

Writers and self-publishers can greatly increase personal income through workshops, seminars and professional speaking engagements. This requires some skill in the area of speaking before a group. This skill can be acquired. Joining a local Toastmasters group (clubs are available in most cities across the United States and Canada) can be a big step in developing poise, power and self-confidence, while speaking on your feet. This supportive organization can help you overcome your fears and teach you how to become a better communicator. Dues are very reasonable, less than $50 per year.

I also strongly recommend you get in touch with my friend, the dynamic Dottie Walters. She is a marvelous woman who is one of the world's best and most inspiring public speakers. Her rise from unskilled housewife to prominent business tycoon (she was president of Hospitality Hostess Services, and had a staff of over 200 hostesses serving the southern California counties of Los Angeles, Orange, San Diego, San Bernardino, and Riverside. Her task force of women welcome a staggering 5,000 new families to Southern California on behalf of 3,000 clients monthly! She recently sold that business to devote all of her time to speaking, writing and publishing. She is nationally recognized as a leading rally speaker, active in the National Speakers Association, and publisher of a speakers' newsletter, *Sharing Ideas Among Speakers*, as well as author/publisher of several books on speaking, sales, and motivation.

219

Dottie has shared the platform with Dr. Norman Vincent Peale, Dr. Robert Schuller, and many other famous speakers, often as the only woman on the program. Dottie is president of three corporations, as well as being a well-known author and speaker. Her book, *Never Underestimate the Selling Power of a Woman,* is a best-selling classic on that subject. (Originally published by Frederick Fell Co., New York, NY and recently reprinted by Melvin Powers, North Hollywood, CA)

Dottie's "Sharing Ideas" is the most exciting and informative news magazine on the subject of speaking for pay. Send only $3 for a sample copy to: Dottie Walters, Royal Publishing, P.O. Box 1120, Glendora, CA 91740.

WRITING AND
THE LAW

Although you don't have to be an attorney at law to be a writer, some knowledge of legal matters can be very helpful. Common sense will usually keep you out of a bind, but here is a crash course in legal matters with which writers often come face-to-face.

How About the Copyright? Be certain you know that the publications for which you intend to write articles or stories are copyrighted before you submit. Always look for the legal copyright notice (©), which usually appears on the title page or at the bottom of the table of contents. If you plan to submit your work to an uncopyrighted publication, you may wish to obtain a copyright yourself. To do this, you produce copies (a few xeroxed copies stapled together of your typewritten copy will do) with the official copyright notice (© 1987 by Russ von Hoelscher, for example), and then register your work with the Copyright office. Request application forms from: Registrar of Copyrights, Library of Congress, Washington, D.C. 20559. After filling out the simple form, you return it, plus two (2) copies of your work and the $10 fee. Uncopyrighted work falls into the *public domain.* In which case, anyone can use it without infringing on the original author's rights.

Rights. You may be able to sell your manuscript many times, depending on what rights you retain or surrender when you make the first sale. Here is a brief description of these "Rights."

1. *First North American Serial Rights.* This allows a periodical to publish your work for the first time in America and Canada. Most publications will realize that you are simply offering them "First time rights" only—the opportunity to publish your work one time only! However, don't take any chances of a misunderstanding. State in writing that you offer *First Rights* only!

2. *Reprint Rights* (or, Second Serial Rights). This allows a publication to reprint your work that has already been published elsewhere. It also allows a periodical to publish part of an already-published book (self-publishers take notice!).

3. *Simultaneous Rights.* Some publications want the whole hog, including TV, movie rights, etc. Be careful here because when you grant "All Rights" you lose all control of your own writing.

Russ von Hoelscher's advice: Keep as many rights as you can. The more rights you hold the better your position regarding future sales.

PROTECT YOUR PROPERTY WITH A COPYRIGHT

Whatever you create on paper, be it a two-page "report" or a 2,000-page literary masterpiece, it is wise to protect your creative labor via the copyright method. This procedure is also simple and easy to obtain.

In 1976, after decades of confusion, the United States Congress updated copyright laws in this nation. Many new provisions were added, giving expanded protection to copyright holders.

Following is a brief, but hopefully, concise review of the new copyright law, plus information on how you can secure a copyright for everything you write.

WHAT IS A COPYRIGHT?

A copyright simply gives you the right to copy, distribute and sell an original work of authorship. It is a law protecting ownership. Generally, a person owns what he or she creates until he sells it, or assigns it to someone else, or until he or she accepts a salary for creating it (publishers often, but not always, hold the copyright). What we call copyright protection is the legal registration of that ownership. The copyright office, for a fee of $10, keeps a record of the date a property existed, to whom it belongs, and has on file in the Library of Congress two copies of the work. In cases of infringement litigation, these data are legal evidences that entitle the owner to obtain redress and collect damages. Copyright protection extends only to *works*; it does *not* extend to any idea, procedure, process, system, etc., regardless of the form in which it is described. That is, you can copyright sequences of words or sounds, of which a copy exists. You copyright the copy, not the content.

A person owns this right to copy only for a specific time. For works created after January 1, 1978, the new law provides a term lasting until the author's death. For works made for hire, and for anonymous and pseudonymous works (unless the author's identity is revealed in Copyright Office records), the new terms will be 75 years from publication or 100 years from creation, whichever is shorter.

Under the old law, the term of copyright was 28 years, plus a second renewal term of 28 years, or 56 years in all. Under the new law, works in their first term must still be renewed, but they can be renewed for a term of 47 years, making a total of 75 years. Copyrights already in their second term at the time the new law went into effect are automatically extended up to the maximum of 75 years without the need for further renewal.

Among other features, the new law also:

• incorporates into a single system proprietary copyright and what was formerly known as common-law copyright (ownership of unpublished works) and provides for the copyrighting of unpublished works;

• establishes guidelines for "fair use" for "purposes such as criticism, comment, news reporting, teaching, (including multiple choices for classroom use), scholarship, or research;"

• creates a Copyright Royalty Tribunal which oversees royalty collections and payments to copyright owners for such uses as in jukeboxes, on public broadcasting, cable TV, etc.

WHAT CAN YOU COPYRIGHT?

Under the new Copyright Act, a claim of copyright is registered under a revised classification system. Instead of the fifteen classes provided under the old law, the new system provides for only five classes. Instead of the numerous application blanks and forms under the old law, the new law provides for only eight. They are:

1. CLASS TX: NON-DRAMATIC LITERARY WORKS. This category is very broad. Except for dramatic works and certain kinds of audiovisual works, Class TX includes all types of published and unpublished works written in words (or other verbal or numerical symbols), such as fiction, nonfiction, poetry, periodicals, textbooks, reference works, directories, catalogs, advertising copy, and the compilations of information.

To secure registration of copyright in this class, one uses application form TX, which replaces six old forms (Form A, Form A-B Foreign, Form A-B Ad Interim, Form B, Form BB, and Form C). You can obtain Form TX, or any copyright form you need, free of charge, by sending a specific request identifying the number of each form you need, to:

Copyright Office
Library of Congress
Washington, DC 20559

2. CLASS PA: WORKS OF THE PERFORMING ARTS. This category includes published and unpublished works prepared for the purpose of being performed directly before an audience or indirectly "by means of any device or process," such as radio or television. The category includes musical works, including any accompanying words; dramatic works, including any accompanying music; pantomimes and choreographic works; and motion pictures and other audiovisual works.

To register your copyright in this category use Form PA,

which replaces four old forms (Form D, Form E, Form E-Foreign, and Form L-M).

CLASS VA; WORKS OF THE VISUAL ARTS. This category consists of published and unpublished works that are pictorial, graphic, and sculptural, including two-dimensional and three-dimensional works of fine, graphic, and applied art, photography, prints and art reproductions, maps, globes, charts, technical drawings, diagrams, and models.

If you wish to copyright a work of visual art, use Form VA, which replaces seven old forms (Form F, Form G, Form H, Form I, Form J, Form K, and Form KK).

4. *CLASS SR: SOUND RECORDINGS.* This category is appropriate for registration for both published and unpublished works in two situations: (1) where the copyright claim is limited to the recording itself; and (2) where the same copyright claimant is seeking to register not only the sound recording but also the musical, dramatic, or literary work embodied in the sound recording. With one exception, "sound recordings" are works that result from the fixation of a series of musical, spoken, or other sounds. This exception is for the audio portions of audiovisual works, such as motion picture soundtracks or audio cassettes accompanying a film strip; these are considered an integral part of the audiovisual work as a whole and must be registered in Class PA. Sound recordings made before February 15, 1972, are not eligible for registration, but may be protected by state law.

Use Form SR to register claim to a Sound Recording.

5. *CLASS RE; RENEWAL REGISTRATION.* This category is used for all renewals of copyrights that were in their first term when the new law went into effect. It covers renewals in all categories. Renewals can only be made in the 28th year of the first copyright registration and have the effect of extending copyright protection for an additional 47 years. Use Form RE for renewal registrations in all categories.

Under the new law, a genuine effort has been made to simplify the categories and red tape surrounding them, as can be seen by the one category/one form norm so far. However, the Copyright Office has found it necessary to create and use three other forms:

Use Form CA to apply for supplementary registration, to correct an error in a copyright registration, or to amplify the information given in a registration.

Use Form IS if you want to import copies of a foreign edition or a non-dramatic literary work that is subject to the manufacturing requirements of section 601 of the new law, which requires with some exceptions and exemptions, that works copyrighted in the United States must be manufactured in the U.S. or Canada.

Use Form GR/CP (for group registration for contributions to periodicals) as an adjunct to a basic application on Form TX, Form PA, or Form VA, if you are making a single registration for a group of works by the same individual author, all first published as contributions to periodicals within a twelve-month period, for example, a group of essays in a travel column, or a series of cartoons (cartoons would be registered in Class VA, visual arts), as provided in section 408(c)(2) of the new law.

In order to qualify for this registration, each contribution must have been published with a separate copyright notice in the name of the copyright owner. This is only a convenience for columnists who wish to register a collection of their work; it does not affect the ownership of the contributions, which belong to the author all along.

A writer does not lose his copyright in a work of authorship by virtue of its being published in a periodical. Article 201 (c), "Contributions to Collective Works," reads: "Copyright in each separate contribution to a collective work is distinct from copyright in the collective work as a whole, and vests initially in the author of the contribution. In the absence of an express transfer of the copyright or of any right under it, the owner of the copyright of the collective work is presumed to have acquired only the privilege of reproducing and distributing the contribution as part of that collective work, any revision of that collective work, and any later collective work in the same series." In other words, unless you agree to something different, a magazine acquires only one-time rights when it publishes a story or article.

STEP BY STEP

To secure a copyright for a published, non-dramatic, literary work, here is what you must do:

First: Publish the work *with the copyright notice.* The law requires that a copyright notice in a specified form "shall be placed on all publicly distributed copies" of the work, on the title page, or (more commonly) on the back side of the title page, or as part of the colophon in a magazine. Use of the copyright notice consists of three elements: (1) the symbol "©" or the word "Copyright," or the abbreviation "Copr."; (2) the year of the first publication; and (3) the name of the copyright owner. For example: "Copyright 1987, Profit Ideas." (Copyrights can be a person's name or a company's name.)

Unlike the old law, the new law provides procedures for correcting errors in the copyright notice, and even for curing the omission of the notice altogether. However, failure to comply with the requirement for copyright notice correctly may result in loss of some areas of valuable copyright protection. If not corrected within five years, you can blow your entire copyright.

Second: Fill out the proper application forms. For a non-dramatic literary work, the proper form would be Form **TX.** Write the Copyright Office for the blanks, then fill them out carefully, using a typewriter or dark ink, after reading the instructions.

Third: Send the required fee, the required copies, and the completed application to "The Registrar of Copyrights, Library of Congress, Washington, DC 20559." The fee for a first copyright of a book is now $10, which must be paid by check or money order made payable to "The Registrar of Copyrights." You are required to deposit two copies of the published work with the Library of Congress (one copy of unpublished works and one copy of contributions to collective works). These are the copies that become evidence in infringement litigation. Send the fee, the copies, and the application together.

When the Registrar of Copyrights has processed your application and filed the copies, you will receive an official certificate of copyright, bearing the official seal of the Copyright Office. That certificate is your evidence of ownership.

Surprising as it may seem, many self-publishers never bother to copyright their work. This is often the case with publishers of small booklets, reports, etc., while some small publishers seem to worry too much about someone "stealing" their precious literary creations. Others seem to worry, not at all, and don't ever bother to copyright.

While it's unlikely another will knock off your information book, manual, etc., word for word, and there is little you can do about them stealing ideas of yours, it's still a good idea to copyright everything you write and publish.

WHEN
THEY WON'T PAY

When you push a pencil or tap typewriter or computer keys for cash and recognition, you must realize most editors are both crazy and incompetent...out to test your level of patience. You've gotta' hang in there and maintain your equilibrium. However, when the push comes to the shove, and your work has been published, but you haven't gotten paid, it's time to get after your just due. Send off two letters—ten days apart. In letter No. 1 remind the editor of his obligation and request immediate action (his check by return mail); in letter No. 2 (make sure this one is sent by registered mail), again ask—make that "demand" payment or suggest you intend to pursue legal action. If no answer comes within ten days, take action! Consult with your attorney and/or file a small claims court suit. Write detailed letters stating your case to the Chamber of Commerce and Better Business Bureau in the publication's home town, and also to the District Attorney in the town of the publication.

Most writers who get the shaft limp away licking their wounds, shedding their tears in their own stale beer. This is stupid! The course of action I have outlined may not always bring satisfying results, but it at least gives you a fighting chance to get what you were promised. You strike a blow for yourself and all your brother and sister free-lancers when you stand up for your rights!

Now don't go off *half-cocked*. Use good judgment. Most editors are overworked and underpaid. As a group they are honest people. You must not confuse delays with fraud. Give the publication the benefit of the doubt, but do go after them hammer and tong once it is evident they plan to stiff you.

GHOST WRITING HELP

If you have a good idea, and a marketing plan for a report, booklet or full-size book (anything from 4 to 400 pages) but don't have the time or desire to write it yourself, my friend, Steve Lockman, of Lancaster, Minnesota can help. Steve is an experienced editor and writer. He offers high quality work at very reasonable rates. Write: Steve Lockman, P.O. Box 137, Lancaster, MN 56735.

WRITING
AND PUBLISHING
RESOURCES

BOOKS

How You Can Make a Fortune Selling Information by Mail, by Russ von Hoelscher. Just recently published and already *the definitive guide* on selling books and other "paper and ink" products (reports, manuals, directories, newsletters, etc.) through advanced mail order promotion methods. The small book you are now reading gives you important insights into making big money selling books by mail. This big new book tells you exactly how to do it, step by step. Now you will learn the *master strategies* and *professional techniques* that maximize mail order bookselling profits. Don't even consider self-publishing and/or mail order bookselling until you own and have read this revealing book, cover to cover. *How You Can Make a Fortune Selling Books by Mail* is available for only $12.95 plus $1.00 postage and handling from: PROFIT IDEAS, 8361 Vickers St., Suite 304, San Diego, CA 92111.

The Self-Publishing Manual, by Dan Poynter. A detailed, highly recommended short course in writing, publishing and selling your own books. This is an important guidebook that deserves your cover-to-cover attention if you intend to self-publish. The new third revised 352-page softcover edition is now available. $14.95 plus $1.00 postage/handling from: PARA PUBLISHING, P.O. Box 4232, Santa Barbara, CA 93101.

232

Book Dealers Dropship Directory, by Al Galasso. Drop-shipping enables you to sell books, collect payment in advance, then have the books shipped direct to your customers from the prime source. You carry no inventory. This directory lists hundreds of reliable dropship publishers. A great source guide! Order now for only $7.00 postpaid from: AMERICAN BOOKDEALERS EXCHANGE, P.O. Box 2525-MM, La Mesa, CA 92041.

How to Sell Books by Mail and Directory of Wholesale Book Sources, by Joseph S. Soukup. Another great manual plus source directory for anyone interested in selling books by mail. Easy to read and easy to use. Order both for only $9.95, postpaid from PROFIT IDEAS, 8361 Vickers St., Suite 304, San Diego, CA 92111.

Writer's Utopia Formula Report (W.U.F.R.), by Jerry Buchanan. First published in 1973, but constantly updated ever since. Loaded with valuable information on how to make real money writing and publishing books, booklets and reports. Written by a man, Jerry Buchanan, who has helped thousands get started in this exciting field. This man teaches from experience, not from a textbook. Highly recommended! Only $10.00 postpaid from: TOWERS CLUB USA, P.O. Box 2038, Vancouver, WA 98661.

BOOK PRINTERS
Paperback or Hardback

Kingsport Press, Inc.
P.O. Box 711
Kingsport, TN 37662

McNaughton & Gunn, Inc.
P.O. Box M-2060
Ann Arbor, MI 48106

R.R. Donnelly & Sons
2223 Martin Luther King Dr.
Chicago, IL 60616

Book-Mart Press, Inc.
2001 Forty-Second St.
North Bergen, NJ 07047

Interstate Book Mfg.
2115 E. Kansas City Rd.
Olathe, KS 66061

Delta Lithograph Co.
14731 Califa St.
Van Nuys, CA 91411

233

OFFSET PRINTERS

To print circulars, brochures, letterheads, etc.

Henry Birtle Co.
1143 E. Colorado St.
Glendale, CA 91205

Big City Litho
550 N. Claremont Blvd.
Claremont, CA 91711

Speedy Printers
23800 Aurora Rd.
Bedford Hts., OH 44146

Trade Rotary
634-D W. Broadway
Glendale, CA 91204

Equitable Web Offset
24 New Bridge Road
Bergen Field, NJ 07621

Fitch Graphics
Box 768500
Atlanta, GA 30328

What information or service do you have that would help a new author to Publish or sell his book? Your help is appreciated

BOOKSELLING AND PUBLISHING ORGANIZATIONS

American Bookdealers
Exchange
P.O. Box 2525
La Mesa, CA 92041

American Booksellers Assoc.
122 E. 42nd St.
New York, NY 10168

American Library Assoc.
50 E. Huron St.
Chicago, IL 60611

The Assoc. of American
Publishers, Inc.
One Park Ave.
New York, NY 10016

The Assoc. of University
Presses
One Park Ave.
New York, NY 10016

COSMEP (Committee of
Small Magazine Editors and
Publishers)
P.O. Box 703
San Francisco, CA 94101

Coordinating Council of
Literary Magazines
Two Park Ave., #1809
New York, NY 10016

Independent Publishers Guide
52 Chepstow Rd.
London W2, Great Britain

Information Publishers
Network
P.O. Box 546
El Cajon, CA 92022

Marin Self-Publishers Assn.
P.O. Box 343
Ross, CA 94957

234

Assoc. of Canadian
Publishers
70 The Esplanade, 3rd Floor
Toronto, ON M5E 1R2

The Authors Guild
234 W. 44th St.
New York, NY 10036

Aviation/Space Writers
Association
21 E. State St., #730
Columbus, OH 43215

Book Publicists of So. Calif.
6430 Sunset Blvd., #503
Hollywood, CA 90028

Bookbuilders of So. Calif.
5225 Wilshire Blvd., #316
Los Angeles, CA 90036

Bookbuilders West
170 Ninth St.
San Francisco, CA 94103

The Christian Booksellers
Association
P.O. Box 200
Colorado Springs, CO 80901

National Assn. of Book
Manufacturers
1730 N. Lynn St.
Arlington, VA 22209

The National Assn. of College
Stores
528 E. Lorain St.
Oberlin, OH 44074

The National Writers Club
1450 S. Havana, #620
Aurora, CO 80012

Poets & Writers, Inc.
201 W. 54th St.
New York, NY 10019

Publishers Marketing Assoc.
2401 Pacific Coast Hwy.
#206
Hermosa Beach, CA 90254

MAGAZINES AND NEWSLETTERS FOR AUTHORS AND PUBLISHERS

Write for a sample copy and current subscription rates.

ALA Booklist
50 E. Huron St.
Chicago, IL 60611

American Bookseller
122 E. 42nd St.
New York, NY 10168

American Libraries
50 E. Huron St.
Chicago, IL 60611

Author's Newsletter
P.O. Box 32008
Phoenix, AZ 85064

Book Dealers World
P.O. Box 2525
La Mesa, CA 92041

Canadian Author & Bookman
P.O. Box 120
Niagara-On-The-Lake, Ont.
Canada LOS IJO

Choice
100 Riverview Center
Middletown, CT 06457
(Undergraduate library market)

The College Store Journal
528 E. Lorain St.
Oberlin, OH 44074

Directions Magazine
Baker & Taylor Co.
1515 Broadway
New York, NY 10036

Editorial Eye
85 South Bragg St.
Alexandria, VA 22312

Forecast Magazine
Baker & Taylor Co.
1515 Broadway
New York, NY 10036

The Horn Book Magazine
Park Square Bldg.
31 St. James St.
Boston, MA 02116

The Huenefeld Report
P.O. Box U
Bedford, MA 01730

IPN Marketing News
P.O. Box 546
El Cajon, CA 92022

Kirkus Reviews
200 Park Ave., South
New York, NY 10033

Library Journal
R.R. Bowker Co.
245 W. 17th St.
New York, NY 10011

I.W.S.
24 Canterbury Rd.
Rockville Centre, NY 11570

Publishers Weekly
R.R. Bowker Co.
245 W. 17th St.
New York, NY 10011

New Pages
4426 South Belsay Rd.
Grand Blanc, MI 48439

Output Mode
P.O. Box 1275
San Luis Obispo, CA 93406

Reference Service Review
P.O. Box 1808
Ann Arbor, MI 48106
(For reference librarians)

San Francisco Review of Books
1111 Kearny St.
San Francisco, CA 94133

School Library Journal
R.R. Bowker Co.
245 W. 17th St.
New York, NY 10011

Selling To Libraries
American Library Assoc.
50 East Huron St.
Chicago, IL 60611

Small Press Magazine
11 Ferry Lane West
Westport, CT 06880

Small Press Review
P.O. Box 100
Paradise, CA 95969

Towers Club-USA
P.O. Box 2038
Vancouver, WA 98668

West Coast Review of Books
8128 Gould Ave.
Hollywood, CA 90046

The Writer
8 Arlington St.
Boston, MA 02116

Writer's Digest
9933 Alliance Road
Cincinnati, OH 45242

Writers Journal
Inkling Publications, Inc.
P.O. Box 65798
St. Paul, MN 55165

BOOK AND OFFICE SUPPLIES

Book Bins, Wire Book Easels,
Book Display Racks, etc.:

The Highsmith Company, Inc.
P.O. Box 800B
Highway 106 East
Ft. Atkinson, WI 53538

All-Purpose Book Counter
Displays and Carriers:

S.L. Enterprises
443 E. Westfield Ave.
P.O. Box 292
Roselle Park, NJ 07204
(201) 245-8440

Beemak Plastics
7424 Santa Monica Blvd.
Los Angeles, CA 90046
(213) 876-1770

Wire Literature Holders
Pegboards, Display Racks:

Siegel Display Products
P.O. Box 95
Minneapolis, MN 55440
(612) 340-1493

Shelf Magazine Files, Desk
Organizers, Communication
Boards, Literature Trays:

Professional Aids
1678 S. Wolf Rd., Suite 90D
Wheeling, IL 60090
(312) 459-6828

Mailing Labels, Cheshire

Mail Supply Co., Inc.
P.O. Box 363
Waukesha, WI 53187

Shipping Bags, Mailing Bags,
Literature & Book Shippers:

Kole Industries, Inc.
P.O. Box 520152
Miami, FL 33152

Binders, Report Covers,
Stationary & Memos,
Business Gifts:

Day-Timers Inc.
Allentown, PA 18001
(215) 395-5884

Loose Leaf Binders:

Vulcan Binder & Cover
P.O. Box 29
Vincent, AL 35178

20th Century Plastics, Inc.
3628 Crenshaw Blvd.
Los Angeles, CA 90051

Office Supplies

Business Envelope Manuf.
900 Grand Blvd.
Deer Park, NY 11729

The Drawing Board
P.O. Box 220505
Dallas, TX 75222

Quill Corp.
P.O. Box 4700
Lincolnshire, IL 60197

Grayarc
P.O. Box 2944
Hartford, CT 06104

Nebs
500 Main St.
Groton, MA 01470

Stationery House
1000 Florida Ave.
Hagerstown, MD 21741

Typesetting

Rush Type
12933 Ha Hana Rd., #7
Lakeside, CA 92040

Typing Service

Steve Lockman
P.O. Box 137
Lancaster, MN 56735

Self-Publishing
Success Seminars

Russ von Hoelscher
P.O. Box 546
El Cajon, CA 92020

SPECIAL REPORTS FOR
WRITERS/PUBLISHERS
(Write for current availability and prices)

P.E.N. American Center
47 Fifth Ave.
New York, NY 10003
(Grants and awards available to
American writers)

The Copyright Office
Office of Public Affairs
Library of Congress
Washington, DC 20559
(General guide to the Copyright Act)

Literature Program
National Endowment for
the Arts
2401 E St. NW
Washington, DC 20506
(Assistance, fellowships and
residencies for writers.)

Federal Trade Commission
Washington, DC 20580
(Shopping By Mail? You're Protected!
FTC Buyer's Guide No. 2
Consumer Alert—The Vanity Press News
release dated 19 July 1959
Vanity Press Findings. Dockets 7005 and
7489)

SECTION FOUR:

How to Make Big Money in Mail Order

Mail order sales are booming! The 1980s have produced unprecedented growth in the direct marketing industry, and the upward trend will continue in the 1990s.

You can start in your spare time and earn as you learn, provided that you have good publications, products or services to offer, and great ads or mailing pieces to do the selling for you.

Since most products or services are bought sight unseen (or only presented with a few small illustrations or photos), your ad copy must be very persuasive. You can make a fortune in mail order today, but only if you are reaching the right market with super ads, and have a smooth mail receiving/shipping system.

This special section of *Stay Home and Make Money* will give you insights into how to operate a successful mail order business.

MAIL ORDER

Mail order is not a business unto itself, rather it is a method of doing business. A gift shop downtown, or a bookstore in a shopping mall are retail stores that rely upon walk-in customers to survive and prosper. The same people who operate these stores could be located in an industrial building, a garage or even at home, selling their novelties, gifts, books or almost any other type of goods or service, using the U.S. mails to conduct their business.

MAIL ORDER IS BOOMING

The growth of the mail order industry during the past few decades has been nothing short of spectacular. Experts are predicting this trend will continue through the 1990s.

YOU CAN START PART TIME

One huge advantage of starting a mail order business is that you can start part time, usually in your own home. This is a big advantage over most commercial businesses that demand full-time attention. Many tens of thousands of Americans and Canadians conduct part-time mail selling ventures while holding a regular job. So can you!

If you're a newcomer to mail order, I strongly advise you to start slow and hopefully learn as you earn. Also, don't expect to make a killing—at least not at first. Mail order selling is exciting and potentially very profitable, but don't expect to get rich by next Tuesday. *The more you learn, the more you'll earn!*

WHAT ABOUT COMPETITION?

You will always face competition. For example: Selling books and reports by mail is one of the most popular forms of mail selling. I estimate over 25% of all mail order business relates to books, reports, magazines, newsletters or some other form of "information" selling. It is a fact—more books, manuals and courses are sold by mail than in the thousands of retail bookstores located across the land. Competition is fierce, but as long as you are offering something new, unique, at a great price, packaged differently, etc., the only real competition you have is yourself. In years gone by, mail order firms used to guard their mailing lists from other firms who sold similar goods. This practice has now gone the way of the dinosaurs. Smart mail order operators sell or swap mailing lists with similar companies, knowing people who buy opportunity books from one company will buy from others. Those who buy hunting and fishing items from one will buy from another. The same with food stuffs, etc. And after buying from your competition, they will still gladly buy something else from you when you have something new or different that they want.

HOW MUCH INVESTMENT IS NEEDED?

While certain opportunity magazines are loaded with ads and stories about how this guy or that one got started in mail order for less than one hundred dollars and earned a fortune, let's keep both feet on the ground. You are reading this in 1987 or 1988 (or beyond), and with prices being what they are, it probably would be fruitless to start a mail order business with less than a couple thousand dollars, and even at that, it would be a modest start.

After all, it will cost several hundred dollars to place even a few little classified ads in national publications; and large display ads can cost anywhere from several hundred to several thousand for one ad in one publication. If you turn to direct mail, you can expect to pay at least $300 to $400 for every 1,000 pieces of mail you send out (the cost of postage, your printed matter, envelopes, etc.), and a 5,000 piece mailing (small by industry standards) will probably cost you close to $2,000.

I would say it will take at least $1,000 or more to "start from scratch," and your chances to get your new venture off the ground, even on a spare-time basis, would be much improved if you have $5,000 to kick things off.

Whatever amount of money you have to invest in your initial mail selling effort, it should be "money that you can live without." You could lose every dime! Am I a prophet of "doom and gloom"? Heck no! In fact, I believe mail order offers the little guy one of his best avenues to success. I believe mail order and the true entrepreneur go together like "bacon and eggs," "love and marriage," "gin and tonic" or whatever other combination turns you on! I also think I should tell you the truth. This method of doing business is not without its risks and pitfalls.

YOUR OWN PRODUCTS OR THOSE FROM OTHER SOURCES?

Most of today's most successful mail order/direct marketing professionals do both. They have control of their own products or services, and also sell related products that they purchase wholesale from other supply sources.

While control over your own merchandise is a desirable goal, if you're starting with limited capital, you have to start by offering products obtained from others.

The drop-ship method (a process that allows you to sell mail order merchandise without handling any stock or doing the actual shipping) is the easiest way to start a mail order business. This is the method I used to get started in this crazy, but rewarding business, over 20 years ago. Dropshipping remains a popular means to sell by mail today. Many of the new dealers who sell my books, manuals and tapes, never carry stock or ship anything.

However, I always recommend to my dealers that they should be purchasing at our low wholesale prices and filling their own orders, if they are using our books as their main offer. With a catalog full of many items, or to obtain follow-up and bounce-back orders, the full dropship method of mail business is fine. However, almost all dropship arrangements only allow a 50-50 split of monies, sometimes even less. This is not usually good enough for long-term success.

To get the 2½ to 1, or bigger markups, you need, you must be able to buy at deep wholesale discounts and/or have control over your own products and services.

WHAT ABOUT MARKUP?

This subject is very subjective. We know of a company in Michigan that sells canoes by mail (like I said, you can sell almost anything via mail order) at about twice the cost it takes to make them. This is a very low markup. However, a custom canoe that may cost one thousand dollars will gross this firm five hundred—a big-ticket item!

We also know another mail dealer in Orange County, California, who sells a mail order "success course" for one hundred dollars a pop and is proud of the fact that his course costs less than $5 to produce. That's a huge markup on a pretty good-sized sale. Another dealer in Los Angeles sells a set of plastic toys for $9.95 that cost him around 50¢ to have made. That, too, is a big markup, but on a relatively low ticket sale.

In between the extremes just mentioned are your normal markup prices. While there is no set rule, I believe you need at least a 2½ to 1 markup. Anything below 2½ is very precarious, and if you can get a ten-to-one markup and still satisfy your customers, so much the better!

246

The amount you charge per unit also depends on many factors, but I would be afraid to handle items that sold for under five dollars each (unless you would be able to offer a variety of small items in your catalog or brochure). If you're using direct mail to make sales, I prefer products and services that bring $20 or more per sale. With the high inflated cost of mailing and/or advertising, you should be hunting for larger ticket items. The days of selling single items priced under $10 appear to be over.

GETTING STARTED ON A SHOESTRING

If you decide to make a small start and "feel your way as you go" in mail order, fine! This can be a great way to launch your new venture. I still think you will need two or three thousand or more to get your business off the ground, but let's face it, how many businesses are there that you could get started for less?

To hold expenditures to bare essentials, you could rent a typewriter (a business must) if you don't already own one. In the beginning, you can type your own letters (if you don't type, you can learn how cheaply at a night school class), do your own addressing and mailing, stock your goods and keep your own records.

A STEP-BY-STEP EXAMPLE OF
A SHOESTRING STARTUP

Let's say you decide to get started in mail order selling books (about one-third of all mail order enterprises are formed around printed matter). Let's say that your full-time occupation is working as an accountant. You believe there are many thousands, even millions, of potential customers for your new book idea, "The Small Business, Easy Bookkeeping and Tax-Saving Kit." You will offer a large manual of record-keeping and tax-saving advice plus, as a bonus, one year's worth of ledgers and forms that a small business can use to easily keep one year's worth of records. Since all printed matter will go into a 3-ring binder and can be printed in single sheets, a local instant printer can handle the small run printing. You decide to only print 250 sets of your manual since you're operating on a shoestring and want to test your creation before making a large cash investment.

A local printer (you checked with three or four to determine the best price at reasonable quality) will give you 250 sets of printed sheets, including forms, gather them, punch three holes in them and put a divider between them, so it will be easy for you to insert in a one-inch binder, all for $1,100. That's $4.25 per unit.

Next, you shop around and find a wholesale stationery store supplier who will furnish you 250 3-ring, one-inch black binders in which the name of your course and your name as author will be silk-screened in imitation gold print on the front cover and the spine at $625 ($2.50 each).

Now, your total productive cost per unit is $4.25 for the printed matter and $2.50 for the 3-ring binder—a cost of $6.75 per unit. In addition, the cost of a padded mailing carton will be 30¢ each, a shipping label will cost you 2¢ and postage costs to mail your package the cheapest method (fourth class book rate) will be $1.32. Since our accountant does business, for now, out of his house and does his own labor (with his wife's help), we won't add very much for any other expenses. There are only a few "extras" (he rents a post office box, uses letterheads, must use shipping tape, office supplies, etc.). We will say all other expenses only add another 20¢ per order.

Now, let's add up per unit:

Printing and binder costs	$6.75
Mailing carton	.30
Shipping label	.02
Postage	1.32
Miscellaneous	.20
Total cost per unit shipped:	$8.59

Our accountant-turned-mail-dealer decides on a price of $39.95 for his tax/bookkeeping kit. Since he has spent approximately two thousand dollars just to print his kits, get the binders and buy various other supplies, he decides he does not want to invest several thousand more in space ads or direct mail at this time. After all, it is his desire to get started on a shoestring, or at least with minimum expense. So he decides on a two-step mail sales program. Small classified ads will be placed in various publications to entice potential customers to write in for more details.

This ad is placed in various business, sales and trade magazines that relate to independent businessmen (among them he could use *Entrepreneur* magazine, *Office* magazine, *American Business, Specialty Salesman, Income Opportunities* and many others).

He selects ten different publications and places this little classified ad:

CUT TAXES TO THE BONE AND USE
WORLD'S SIMPLEST, MOST EFFECTIVE
BOOKKEEPING SYSTEM. FREE DETAILS.
NAME AND ADDRESS

This is nine selling words plus six more for address purposes. 15 words.

His total investment is $375 to place ten ads, since the publications he picked average out at about $2.50 per word for classified ads. Each ad is keyed so that he can check results. To key, he simply tagged a key on to his post office box. Example:

American Business Ad, Box 100-AB

Entrepreneur, Box 11-ET

If he had used a street address, he would have keyed like this:

101-AB Elm Street

Since this gentleman is an accountant by profession, he knows the value of keeping good records (something all mail dealers must do), and he charts the inquiry and sales received from his classified ad and uses the effective follow-up mailing system.

EFFECTIVE TWO-STEP MAIL SELLING

- Every inquiry receives a four-page advertising brochure, a publisher's letter, order card and return envelope.

- All inquiries are sent this literature the same day or next day after the inquiry comes in.

- Using a predated mail system (all one needs for this is several baskets or boxes), a follow-up mailing is made 15 days after the first mailing, if no order is obtained.

- A second follow-up (the third mailing) goes out 15 days from the second (30 days from the original mailing), if no order has been obtained.

While some dealers will mail 4, 5 or 6 times to an original inquiry, I have found it unprofitable to mail beyond three times (an original and two follow-ups) unless dealing with a high-ticket sales item (over $50).

Here's what the test on the tax and record-keeping classified ad program may look like 90 days (when 90% of results should be in!) after the ads appear:

	Inquiries	Sales
Publication A	60	3
B	52	2
C	40	0
D	30	5
E	48	5
F	34	1
G	27	2
H	20	6
I	25	3
J	15	1
	351	28

250

That's about an 8% sales-to-inquiry ratio. However, as always can be expected, results were not uniform in these publications. The top three (A, B and C) pulled 152 inquiries but only five orders, a less than 2.5% yield to what seem to be qualified inquiries (remember, on the two-step, they write you and ask for more information, as opposed to direct mail, where you are probably going out cold). The real breadwinners here were D and H. These two publications did not bring a ton of inquiries (50), but those 50 inquiries nailed 11 orders, a great 22% inquiry-to-order ratio. "H" was the big bread winner—6 orders per 20 inquiries—a fantastic 30% conversion rate.

CHECKING PROFITS

Now, let's check into whether our new venture showed a profit first time up to bat.

We will put our cost at 28¢ (quite low) each time we send out our mailing piece (the 4-page brochure, sales letter, order card and return envelope, all enclosed in an outer envelope.

It took a total of 1,012 mailings over 90 days to generate 28 orders at $39.95 each. Why 1,012 mailings, you ask? Here's a realistic breakdown:

First Mailing: 351

Second Mailing: 334

Third Mailing: 327

These statistics indicate we received 17 out of 28 orders within 15 days of the first mailing. Thus, we made a follow-up mailing to our 351 inquiries, minus the 17 who ordered, or a total of 334. Within 15 days of our second mailing we had received 7 more orders, so we mailed the third and final mailing (second follow-up) to 327 and picked up 4 additional orders.

A total of 1,012 mailings (of course, we did not do all our mailing and remailing at once, but rather over three months' time. Nevertheless, the numbers are the same).

Now, we can compute all costs:

Advertising cost for small classified, run once each in ten publications	$375.00
Cost to mail and remail to inquiries, a total of 1,012 mailings at 28¢ ea.	$283.36
Cost to fulfill orders, 28 orders at $8.59 ea.	$240.52
TOTAL COST	$898.88

Against this deficit, we add the money we generated from this venture...

That's easy! 28 orders at $39.95 = $1,118.60

Deducting $898.88 total costs from $1,118.60 revenue generated, we have left a modest profit of $119.72. Now, if you place a dollar value on your time (and you should!) and perhaps allow for one or two returns (no matter how good your products or services are, you can't please everyone), chances are our accountant-turned-mail-order-entrepreneur did little more than break even. That still would be okay. He has a mailing list of over 1,000 "business people," including 28 prime buyers. More important, he has tested ten magazines and separated those that will work for this particular offer (no two offers are alike).

In this example, publications "D", "E", "H" and "I" would certainly be worth more insertions of the ad used. Publications "A" and "G" may warrant re-testing this or another ad (it is wise to test several different, small ads). The others did not work well at all and probably should be dropped.

252

Your whole space advertising campaign, be it classifieds, small space ads or large space ads, is a process of "keep or throw away." Constant testing proves certain publications to be good media for your ads and eliminates others who do not pull for you.

Using direct mail, the same process is repeated, except you are proving or disproving mailing lists.

In addition, to be successful you need strong advertising literature. The best media or mailing list needs eye-catching, order-getting to generate business.

MAIL ORDER SPACE ADVERTISING

Now we will direct our attention to direct response space ads. While two-step inquiry advertising, mainly using small classifieds to generate many inquiries for followup literature, is often the best cost-effective form of advertising (with the exception of free advertising and publicity), nothing can beat a profitable space advertising campaign for *no strain, no pain, nice and easy profits!* Sweet it can be, easy to make it work big, it is not!

TESTING AND PERFECTING

If you're eager to make direct response advertising pay off big for the book or report you're peddling, you better start testing. An independent publisher can get an inquiry ad campaign off the ground for only a few hundred dollars; not so with space advertising. I usually advise my clients that no less than *five thousand* will be required to test display ads. Some advertisers commit many times that amount just for testing purposes. Example: If you have a money-making business opportunity book or report to sell, sales and opportunity magazines like *Opportunity, Success Opportunities, Income Opportunities, Selling Direct,* and *Moneymaking Opportunities* are good space ad media. Full page ads (usually the most productive and overall best ad size) in all five of these fine publications would cost you over $14,000 for a one-time insertion in each. Sure you could choose just one of them for your test, but results would not be conclusive and you would still have to plunk down around $3,000.

Without exception, the pro tests and tests some more until a big ad clicks. When the orders begin coming in at a sure-fire profitable flow, the direct order promoter rolls out, buying all the ad space (inside acceptable media geared to the offer) that is available at "reasonable" rates.

INFLATED AD RATES

Since there isn't too much in the way of "reasonable" or "low cost" advertising out there, we must have the *right book,* the *right price* and the *right kind of readers..* Nobody ever said it would be easy, but inflated ad rates (double for most publications in the past five years while the readership numbers have generally stayed the same or only seen minor increases) have made space a difficult place to hang out in. It is estimated only one out of every fifteen space ads tested click and warrant *rolling out!*

THE BEST MONTHS TO RUN DISPLAY ADS (SPACE ADS) FOR MOST MAIL ORDER ITEMS

While mail order gift catalog houses often list the last four months of the year (September through December) as their best mail order season, I have found that this is not true for the majority of mail order sellers. Over twenty years of promoting my own books and many other products as well as helping many others promote theirs, has given me the following seasonal mail sales information.

In addition to giving you the most desirable months (January and February are the very best!), I have assigned a percentage value.

(1) January	100%
(2) February	96%
(3) September	91%
(4) October	87%
(5) March	82%
(6) August	80%
(7) November	75%
(8) July	73%
(9) April	70%
(10) May	64%
(11) June	60%
(12) December	59%

My records indicate the same ad (it's important that we compare an apple to an apple) in January or February will pull 40% more orders than the ad would receive if run in June or December. That could easily be the difference between success and failure! While I believe in remaining active year 'round, I also increase my advertising and mailing in the fall and winter, August through March, with the exception of December.

Your own information offer and your own tests for same may vary slightly from my listing of most favorable (January) to least desirable (December) months, but overall, I think you'll discover my charts are quite accurate, unless you sell gift items. Gift items always sell best from early in September right on to Christmas Day.

DON'T CONFUSE COVER DATE
WITH ON SALE DATE

While newspapers will be able to run your ads a few days after you buy them (this makes them a favorite fast test medium), monthly and bi-monthly magazines often require your copy three months in advance. Aside from the long wait, the advertiser must understand the on-sale vs. cover date scheme. Example: September signals the start of the new mail order book selling season. It is a pretty good month to test the direct response pull of your new report, manual,

255

book, newsletter, etc., **but watch out!** If you buy a September cover in almost any leading monthly newsstand magazine, you're going to be in the mails and sitting on the magazine racks in July or August. Two of the worst pulling months! Check your "on sale" date. It is far more vital than the one printed on the front cover of the publication. The majority of magazines go on sale 4 to 8 weeks prior to what the cover says. Try to find a May *Playboy* in May, no way—unless you go to a second-hand shop. By mid-May, the May and June issues have both been taken off the racks and the July issue holds sway. So it is with most leading monthlies.

EFFECTIVE PRINT MEDIA

Here is a list of some effective space advertising media based on my own personal experience as a book promoter, copywriter and advertising consultant, along with the shared knowledge of others. Needless to say, this is subjective information. Many excellent publications have not been tested. I can only state those listed have proved effective for some of my (certainly not all) direct response ads.

The following have proven their effectiveness! For convenience I have divided them into classifications (classifications are entirely my own and may not always fully represent the publications).

SUPERMARKET TABLOIDS

National Enquirer
Globe
The Star
National Examiner

GENERAL MAIL ORDER

Cappers Weekly
Grit
Moneysworth
American Business
Better Living

SALES & OPPORTUNITY

Success Opportunities
Selling Direct
Moneymaking Opportunity
Income Opportunity
Spare Time
Entrepreneur
In Business
Personal Selling Power

GAMBLING/
HORSE RACING

Daily Racing Form
Gambling Times
Turf & Sports Digest
Winning

ASTROLOGY/OCCULT

Your Astrology
Fate
Beyond Reality
UFO Report
Psychic

DAILY NEWSPAPERS

USA Today
L.A. Times
Detroit Free Press
Des Moines Register
Philadelphia Enquirer
L.A. Herald-Examiner
San Francisco Examiner
Rocky Mt. News
Chicago Tribune
Houston Post
Dallas Morning News

SUNDAY
NEWS SUPPLEMENTS

USA Weekend
Parade

SPORTS

Sport
Sporting News
Sports Special Group

SCIENCE & MECHANICS

Popular Science
Popular Mechanics
Family Handyman
Science & Mechanics

OUTDOOR-TYPE

Sports Afield
Field & Stream
Outdoor Life
Fins & Feathers

WOMEN'S MAGAZINES

McCall's Needlework
Family Circle
Cosmopolitan
True Confessions Group
House Beautiful
Better Homes & Gardens
New Woman
Parents' Magazine
Redbook
Woman's Day

SPECIAL INTEREST

Wall St. Journal
VFW Magazine
Detective Group
Herald-Tribune
    Crossword Group
Hit-Parader
Treasure
DC Comic Group
Marvel Comic Group
New Age
Prevention
Writers Digest
Mother Earth News
Spotlight

Well, that's a thumbnail sketch of some effective mail order media. All of the above publications accept display ads and most also accept classifieds. I have chosen not to include ad rates here, as ad rates are forever changing (going up!!). Write for most recent rate cards on your letterhead and request a sample copy. Nearly all of the above leading publications will send a sample with their ad rates.

DIRECT MAIL
ADVERTISING

The recent increases in the U.S. Postal rates have had little effect on the current boom in direct mail advertising. In fact, leading mailing houses report new clients and increased business on all fronts.

Direct mail is the third largest advertising medium in the country, just behind newspapers and television. It is, perhaps, an unknown sleeping giant. In the ten years, from 1977 to 1987, direct mail advertising more than doubled, with an increase of 115%! Experts expect direct mail volume to triple during the decade of the 1990s.

Direct mail serves an important function, and it is a vital direct marketing vehicle. It is also on the increase. In fact, if you subscribe to any major news magazine or other leading national journal, you can be sure that you will continue to receive quite an assortment of unsolicited mail. They rent your name along with thousands of others' names to buyers who want to reach you.

There's a growing awareness in all marketing areas of the effectiveness of direct mail advertising.

There are many good lists now available for all types of merchandise and direct mail campaigns. While no one should automatically discount the potential profits available from display, direct order or classified inquiry advertising, the self-publisher ought to investigate the possibility of going after his/her readership via direct mail. Many dealers are using both space advertising and direct mailings.

ALMOST INSTANT RESULTS

The mail order dealer who places display or classified ads in monthly magazines may have to wait three or four months to evaluate the results of such advertising. Most publications now require ad copy six to ten weeks before the magazine is published. After publication of a monthly magazine, you're still looking at five or six weeks before you can make a judgement on total effectiveness of the media. Compared to this delay, direct mail is lightning fast! Certainly you'll spend a little time preparing copy for your circulars or brochures, but once the mailing is made, you'll know the results in just a few weeks. Approximately 90% of total results will "be in" within five weeks. In little more than one month, chances are you'll have almost every reply you're going to get. A few late orders may straggle in over several months' time, but this "drag" will be quite small—usually less than 3% of total volume.

GOOD COPY A MUST

It takes good advertising copy to sell books or other products and services through space advertising or direct mail.

Space advertising in newspapers or magazines demands "tight copy." By this I mean, every word has to pack a wallop. Space is at a premium, and even in a large display ad, the ad copy must be concise. While no words should be wasted in a direct mailing piece, it is possible and often advisable to use two or three times as many "words" to get your message across. A four-page 8½x11 brochure, folded with an order form, a sales letter, and return envelope, often makes a responsive mailing piece.

259

MAILING LISTS

You can have a great mail order product or service to offer. You can add to it sizzling ad copy, and you still could fail. Direct mail professionals repeat over and over, "the mailing list is numero uno" in importance! Good copy is a close second, but nothing is more vital than your mailing list.

If you're selling a book on astrology, you better be aiming your mailings at people interested in astrology or at least an updated occult sciences mailing list, not merely to general book buyers. If you're selling a great new "fishing plug," you must be mailing to specialized lists of fishermen/sportsmen, not merely to "novelty gift buyers," etc. You must use the rifle, not shotgun, approach and zero in on your market.

12 DIRECT MAIL SUCCESS TIPS

(1) DO YOU REALLY KNOW WHO YOU'RE TRYING TO REACH WITH YOUR MAILING? If not, you had better find out. You must use the highest quality names available—the right persons for your offer. Remember, it is not the quantity of the names you use that counts; it is the quality.

(2) DOES YOUR SERVICE OR PRODUCT MEET THE EXPECTATIONS OF YOUR TARGET GROUP? Have you produced or chosen the right product for your market or the right market for your product?

(3) IS YOUR AD COPY TAILOR-MADE TO YOUR POTENTIAL CUSTOMERS? When you are certain your product matches well with your lists, it is vital that you create a mailing piece that fits well with the two and appeals more to the emotions than the intellect. People spend ten times more money on their emotions than what their intellect dictates. Mailings aimed at emotions have the best chance for big success.

(4) IS YOUR MAILING PIECE STRONG BUT SIM-PLE? Does it (A) correctly fit the "interest" of your potential customers and (B) is it clear and direct? Make it too complicated and most people will do nothing. Keep it lean, clean and simple and many will order. The reader must understand your offer fully.

(5) IS YOUR COPY SINCERE? It may take hard-hitting copy to get the orders, but your copy must also be sincere and believable. Most people are skeptical when they receive a direct mailing, especially if your company is not known to them. It takes sincere and direct-written communication to dissolve doubt and motivate confidence in placing an order.

(6) DO YOUR GRAPHICS FIT YOUR COPY? Don't go "graphic crazy": a picture or two and a couple of appropriate illustrations could enhance your mailing piece; too much use of graphics or uncalled use of photos or illustrations will only distract. Composition, copy and illustration must be integrated and blend well together.

(7) ARE YOU WORKING WITH THE CLOCK, NOT AGAINST IT? You must be willing to spend enough time planning your mailings, and you must give yourself enough time to do the job well. If you find yourself mailing the first of December a mailing you "planned" November first, you need to coordinate your time and plan your mailings better.

(8) ARE YOU GETTING THE MOST FROM YOUR MAILING PROGRAM? Have you checked every detail? Is your mailing piece as ready as you can make it? Here I am not talking about the copy itself or even the overall format but those "little details" that can be very crucial. Have you been spot-checking your printing to be sure quality is sharp throughout? Is the order blank easy to fill in? Is it simple? Etc. All the intricate details need constant checking. Don't leave anything to chance.

(9) IS YOUR FULFILLMENT DEPARTMENT STREAMLINED? It is one thing to get the order, quite another to keep your customer happy. There is no room in

direct mail selling for a bottleneck in your order department. You must monitor results here continuously. Orders must be promptly processed and filled, hopefully with 24 hours.

(10) ARE YOU INCLUDING STRONG "BOUNCE BACK" ORDERS? Sharp direct mailers know they can receive up to a 10% return with a strong "bounce back" offer. When buyers are pleased with the original offer they have purchased, they are more than willing to send you another order on a "package stuffer offer" that appeals to them. Since these bonus sales cost very little to procure, they should be an important part of your mail order program.

(11) ARE YOU ESTABLISHING A LONG-TERM CON-TINUITY WITH YOUR BUYERS? Your own customer list is by far your greatest potential source of revenue. It will usually outpull cold lists by a two-to-one or three-to-one margin. You must develop new offers continuously, even if you must deal through other supply sources. It is important that you work (mail to) your customer list at least three or four times per year.

(12) IS YOUR WHOLE APPROACH TO DIRECT MAIL SET UP FOR MAXIMUM RESULTS? Before and beyond your direct mailings, is your entire set-up moving forward in a positive fashion? Do you work closely with printers and other suppliers? Are you in close contact with mailing list brokers? Do you sell or trade your customer name list to obtain full benefits? Is every aspect working smoothly? If there are a few snags, get busy oiling them. Direct mail selling can be so very profitable, but all systems, primary and backup, must be kept in smooth-working order.

THE PROVEN
DIRECT MAIL FORMAT

Your imagination is really your only limitation in designing a direct mail package. However, the following direct mail format has withstood the test of time, and repeatedly proven itself to be effective in the majority of direct mail efforts.

Letters

1. First in importance in the direct format is the letter (remember: direct mail is supposed to be one-to-one, personal advertising). The letter can be one page or many pages. The key is to use as many words as needed to sell your offer, but no more than necessary. Keep it friendly, personal, enthusiastic, with an easy to swallow hard sell, and *do* ask for the order.

2. The standard and proven mailing piece consists of an outside envelope, letter, circular, order card and reply envelope.

3. All important sentences should be highlighted by bold type, caps, italics or underlining.

4. A two or four-page letter almost always has more pulling power than a one-page letter. In some cases (especially high-ticket newsletter subscription offers and home-study courses) extremely long letters (up to 8 pages and more) have proven themselves to be very, very effective. It's said, *Nobody has time to read long advertising sales letters, and yet they usually are the ones which bring home the most mail orders.* Think about it!

5. A neatly typed "personal style" letter is more effective than a professional-looking typeset letter. Everything in your letter should come across as one-to-one communication.

Circulars

1. A professional-looking circular (typeset with photos and/or art work) is usually the best way to support a personalized letter that contains no photos or art work.

2. The more expensive your offer is, the more professional-looking your circular (but not your letter) should be.

3. Use several "testimonials." If possible, use full names, because they are much more effective than the use of just initials.

Outside Envelopes

1. While a combination of larger or smaller sizes of envelopes have proven to be effective for various offers, the standard size No. 10 works best for most.

2. Teaser copy that relates to the copy inside usually, but not always, will increase response. Only individual tests will determine this.

Reply Envelopes

1. Any reply envelopes increases results.

2. Postage-free reply envelopes will often out-pull those that require your customer to affix a stamp.

Order Card or Form

1. A separate order form will usually out-pull one that is printed on your circular that needs to be cut out.

2. An order form with an "official-looking" guarantee will usually out-pull one that simply states a guarantee.

Postage

1. Postage-metered envelopes will out-pull a preprinted permit. Individual postage stamps slow down the mailing operation, but usually are most effective.

2. There is often little difference in pull between first class or bulk rate. However, if you use first class, always use a big, bold type to let the receiver know he is receiving a **FIRST CLASS** mailing. Never, never use a preprinted first class permit on your envelopes. If you do that, you are paying first class postage rates, while making your outer envelope appear to be a bulk-rate mailing. That's not being very smart.

My most important advice for your direct mail package (as it was in placing space ads) is to load up everything (the sales letter, the brochure or circulars, the lift letter—if you use one—and the order card) with "tons" of benefits.

FINDING PRODUCTS TO SELL

If you are going to self-publish your own book or report, or have your own invention you are developing, you will have a *primary product*. If not, you must contact other supply sources. While good mail order products are available from a large variety of suppliers, manufacturers, big distributors, closeout sources, importers, and publishers are among the major sources of supply.

Closeouts can offer you super markups. Check the classified section of large metropolitan newspapers for bargain merchandise, plus industry journals. Also frequent swapmeets and flea markets looking for items that may be turned into hot mail order sellers.

Importers can be found in the "white pages" of big city phone directories. You may wish to also consider importing your own special products. Unusual items from far away places have brought riches to several mail dealers. Your local branch office of The Department of Commerce maintains many books and trade journals on importing and exporting. You'll be surprised on the storehouse of knowledge available from this government agency. These people know the world trade business and are ready, able, and very willing to help you. You can prosper by taking advantage of their many productive services. Best of all, this help is free! Anyone anxious to get involved in importing products must be willing to study everything available on how to make money in this exciting and rewarding field.

If you want to sell "paper and ink" products, only do

business with publishers who are willing to offer you good markups. You must double your money on any dropship selling arrangements, and you need 2½ to 1, or better, markups when you purchase wholesale from publishers.

RECOMMENDED BOOKS

How to Start and Operate a Mail-Order Business, by Julian L. Simon. This book, now in a fourth edition, has become a classic. Absolutely loaded with both creative and common sense advice on how to get started right and successfully operate a mail order business. This valuable guidebook has helped thousands mine the mail order goldmine. Highly recommended. The newly published 4th edition (1987) is available for $34.95 plus $2.00 postage/handling, from: McGraw-Hill Book Co., 1221 Avenue of the Americas, New York, NY 10020.

How I Made A Million Dollars In Mail Order, and other works by E. Joseph Cossman. We all have guides or mentors that have inspired us and helped put us on a specific path. My spiritual mentor is the late great Ernest Holmes. Dr. Holmes is the founder of Religious Science and the author of dozens of illuminating books, including the powerful spiritual classic, *The Science of Mind.* My business/mail order mentor is E. Joseph Cossman. His best-selling book was instrumental in my decision 20 years ago to launch a mail order/direct marketing career. Thanks again, Joe. For information on how you can order this recently updated *mail order success bible* or Joe's marvelous complete wealth-building home study course of cassette tapes and instruction manuals, the best information of its kind available, write directly to Joe for free information, Cossman International, Inc., P.O. Box 4480, Palm Springs, CA 92263.

SOURCES

RECOMMENDED READING

How to Achieve Total Success, by Russ von Hoelscher. "Total Success" gives you 442 pages of knowledge on how you can have more success, money, love, health and happiness. The *Mind Science* techniques in this powerful manual can transform your life into a new, rich and rewarding experience. "It might have been" will vanish from your vocabulary. A "must own and use" book for any man or woman who wants to define and achieve great upcompromising success. Only $12.95 plus $1.00 postage/handling from: Profit Ideas, 8361 Vickers St., Suite 304, San Diego, CA 92111.

Secrets Of The Millionaires, by George F. Sterne. This great wealth-building book, written by a self-made millionaire shows how dozens and dozens of ordinary people became rich, and how you can too. In addition to *Sterne's Success Secrets*, you'll discover the million dollar success strategies of many of today's most successful entrepreneurs (W. Clement Stone, Charles Schwab, Joseph Sugarman, Richard Thalheimer, Jane Evans, Dottie Walters, Nido Qubein, Mo Siegel and many others). *Secrets Of The Millionaires* is a one-of-a-kind book. It can teach you how to get very rich. Only $12.95 plus $1.00 postage/handling from: Profit Ideas, 8361 Vickers St., Suite 304, San Diego, CA 92111.

Small-Time Operator, by Bernard Kamoroff, C.P.A. This is one of the finest books ever written and published on the "Mechanics" of running a successful, small business. *How to get started right and stay on target; how to set up books and record-keeping system; how to deal effectively with employees; handle your tax responsibilities, and a whole lot more.* The subject matter may appear dull, albeit necessary, but Mr. Kamoroff has accomplished the ultimate for a book of this nature. His information is crucial, and his writing style makes it come to life and capture our interest. Only $9.95 plus $1.00 from: Bell Springs Publishing, P.O. Box 640, Laytonville, CA 95454.

The Unabashed Self-Promoters Guide, by Dr. Jeffrey Lant. Subtitled: *What Every Man, Woman, Child and Organization in America Needs to Know About Getting Ahead by Exploiting the Media.* This is a totally unique, "must own" rare and valuable book. I think any person going into business, any kind of business, large or small, who does not buy it, read it, and use its illuminating contents is very foolhardy. This is the best book on the vital subject of low-cost, high-explosive self-promotion. You will learn the prerequisites for totally successful self-promotion, how to approach the media, how to put together your own dazzling media kit, plus much more. The price for Dr. Lant's large 8½x11 softback manual is $29.95 plus $1.50 for postage/handling from: Publishers Media, P.O. Box 546, El Cajon, CA 92022.

The Consultant's Kit, by Dr. Jeffrey Lant. If you have a skill or are developing a service and would like to establish a profitable consulting practice, this masterful manual was written for you. Not only is Dr. Lant one of America's most successful consultants, he knows how to teach others his unique business-building techniques. There is big money available to today's entrepreneur consultant and this big book tells you exactly what you must do to reap the rich rewards. At $29.95 plus $1.50 postage/handling it's not expensive, just essential to anyone who wants to profit in the advice business. Order from: Publishers Media, P.O. Box 546, El Cajon, CA 92022.

How To Succeed As An Independent Consultant, by Herman Holtz. This is another excellent book on making money as a free-lance consultant. An extremely valuable guide to the technical, business and promotional aspects of successful consulting. A real value at only $19.95 plus $1.50 postage/handling from: John Wiley and Sons, Inc., 605 Third Ave., New York, NY 10158.

The Smart Way to Buy a Business, by John C. Kohl, Sr., and Atlee M. Kohl. This book provides potential business buyers with questions that must be asked so that intelligent decisions can be made. This concise guidebook will help a prospective buyer work systematically through the complete business acquisition process. You can order a copy of this hardback manual for $19.95 postpaid, from: Woodland Publishers, 3007 Skyway Circle North, Irving, TX 75038.

IMPORTANT DIRECTORIES

Directory of Leading Magazines and Newspapers. A great source of approximately 300 U.S. newspapers and almost 600 most popular consumer and trade magazines. Names, addresses and current circulation. Whether for advertising purposes or as a source of free publicity, this new directory will help you reach millions of buyers for any product, service or book you wish to promote. Only $12 postpaid from: Publishers Media, Box 546, El Cajon, CA 92022.

Book Dealers Dropship Directory, by Al Galasso. Dropshipping enables you to sell books, collect payment in advance, then have the books shipped direct to your customers from the prime source. You carry no inventory. This directory lists hundreds of reliable dropship publishers. A great source guide! Order now for only $7 postpaid from: American Bookdealers Exchange, P.O. Box 2525-MM, La Mesa, CA 92041.

The Directory of Wholesale Printing and Office Supplies. You can slash up to 50% off your printing and office supply costs by securing a copy of the latest edition of "Directory of Wholesale Printing and Office Supply Sources." This super directory is loaded with great wholesale sources that can save you a bundle on office supplies and mail order printing. Only $9.95 postpaid from: A.I.M., Dept. WP, P.O. Box 22822, San Diego, CA 92122.

SPECIAL PUBLICATION OFFERS

Publishers Media (P.O. Box 546, El Cajon, CA 92022) has many back issues of Russ von Hoelscher's *Freelance*, and *Words for Wealth* newsletters available. Good information for mail order booksellers and/or anyone thinking about self-publishing a book or manual. Special! 6 issues (a reg. $18 value) for only $5 postpaid.

Book Dealers World is the Direct Mail Marketplace for Book Dealers, Writers, Dropshippers, and Independent Publishers. Each issue is loaded with valuable publishing-book selling information from editorial director Al Galasso, and many of today's most creative minds, including: Dr. Jeffrey Lant, Cynthia Schubert, Bev Harris, David Bendah and Russ von Hoelscher. This is a most worthwhile publication. Just $2.00 will get you a sample copy from: American Bookdealers Exchange, Dept. BDW, P.O. Box 2525, La Mesa, CA 92041.

International Wealth Success is a unique mail order monthly business opportunities newsletter covering capital sources, finder's fees, real estate, getting started in mail order, import-export, quick methods for raising money, venture capital, etc. Subscribers are entitled to run 12 free ads per year in the newsletter. Every issue is at least 16 pages and includes real-life experiences from Beginning Wealth Builders who are making their fortune today. Sample copy only $1.00. I.W.S., Inc., 24 Canterbury Rd., Rockville Centre, NY 11570.

Sharing Ideas is a very special news magazine published by our friend, world-class professional speaker, Dottie Walters. Dottie shows writers/publishers how they can make lots of extra money in the fascinating world of speaking for pay. Each big (up to 48 pages or more) issue is crammed with vital information. Sample copy only $3.00 from: Royal Publishing, Box 1102, Glendora, CA 91740.

Two Good Business Newsletters Have Become One Great One! The Shoestring Marketer and the Small Business Marketer have merged. The new title for the publication is *Shoestring Marketer Newsletter.* This newsletter is overflowing with great, low-cost marketing ideas. Get your sample copy for only $2 from *Shoestring Marketer Newsletter,* P.O. Box 1389, Yuba City, CA 95992.

FREE GOODIES

Write on your letterhead to receive free magazines, reports, etc.

Opportunity Magazine
6 N. Michigan Ave.
Chicago, IL 60602
Free subscription to this business-opportunity magazine

Money Making Opportunities
11071 Ventura Blvd.
Studio City, CA 91604
Free subscription to this business opportunity magazine

Selling Direct
6255 Barfield Rd.
Atlanta, GA 30328
Free subscription to this business opportunity magazine

DM News
19 W. 21st St.
New York, NY 10010
Free subscription to this direct marketing/mail order tabloid

Innovative Marketing
P.O. Box 22822
San Diego, CA 92122
Free report on "Multi-Level Marketing"

Pitney-Bowes, Inc.
Walnut & Pacific Sts.
Stamford, CT 06904
How to Put More Personality into Your Business Letters Booklet

273

A.B. Dick Co.
5700 W. Touhy Ave.
Chicago, IL 60648
How to Plan & Publish a
Mimeographed Newsletter
Booklet

Dinner & Klein
P.O. Box 3814
Seattle, WA 93814
How to Develop, Maintain
and Use Profitably Your Own
Mailing Lists Report

COSMEP
P.O. Box 703
San Francisco, CA 94101
Free small publisher's
newsletter